THE CHAIRS

POEMS BY
N. M. HOFFMAN

PAINTINGS BY
GLORIA MATUSZEWSKI

THE CHAIRS

POEMS BY

N. M. HOFFMAN

PAINTINGS BY

GLORIA MATUSZEWSKI

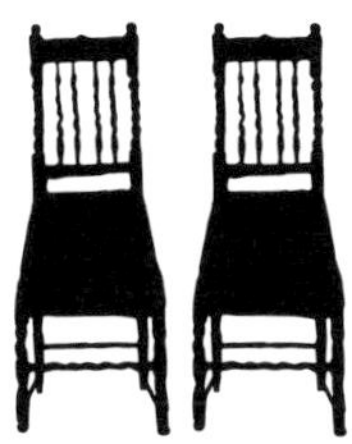

KH&W

KEARNS, HOWARD & WALKER

2024

PREFACE & ACKNOWLEDGMENTS
from the Poet

What the Place Is From Where to See

In works of philosophy, the Chair lives large as what is "real" for purposes of intellectual investigations of reality. We see this on the stages of philosophical discourse from Plato to Wittgenstein to Baudrillard, without putting too fine a point on it. This Chair of philosophy is here wedded to the Chair as a speaking thing, an intimacy generated from a long study of Rilke's poems, *The Roses,* with their controlled precision of focus.

Before acknowledging the inspiration of the paintings of Gloria Matuszewski for these Chair poems, I would like to thank the team at Kearns, Howard & Walker for making this publication what it is in the world. This includes Kathleen Brown (author of *Bewilderness: Reality Fiction Bred While Working in Animal Shelters* and Chair of the Advisory Board of KH&W), and Board Advisors Barbara Alderson, Karen Ann, Bradford C. Bennett, Kamala Friedman, Jeffrey Gersten, Laraine Gladstone, Catherine S. Holder and Betty Zielinski. Their interest and enthusiasm, along with that of many other members of the Tai Chi family of Hubert H. and Elsie Lui, have been invaluable, not only for the life of this book, but also for the support of my poetry, of Gloria's work and of our collaborations of poetry and paintings over many years.

I also would like to acknowledge the ever-presence of my family: those cousins and siblings and their children who are always there for me, in particular my sisters Mary Estrella, Carol Hoffman-Budde and Jane Esposito and my brother, Charles Hoffman, and their spouses respectively, Bruce Estrella, Fred Hoffman-Budde, Gary Esposito and Sally Vriesma Hoffman, each one too dear even for words.

Gloria and I work often *in tandem*, which is the interchange of ideas by which we link certain poems and paintings as we continue in our respective directions. After our work *in tandem* on *The Roses* book, Gloria began to paint images of Chairs and I was bereft of the sisterly grounding of paintings that Gloria's rose images had afforded me while I was working on the Rilke project. This led me to the viability of following Gloria along the path of the Chair images by exploring the powerful Rilkean conception of the *Dinggedicht* ("object poem" or "thing poem"), so closely observed in translating *The Roses*, to approach my own poetry with respect to the Chair.

Thus the whole poetic enterprise in this present work of poetry and paintings is comprised of a gesture toward a method observed in translating Rilke's *Roses* that for me was simultaneously manifest in Gloria's commanding visions of the Chair. The paintings in this book magnify the specificities of reality that I leaned into as a poet learning from the master poet, Rilke, to control, perhaps better said, to actually see reality by means of a programmatic method first observed in *The Roses*.

And yet one poet's method is another poet's floor. From a focus on the *thing*, that is, the Chair as arbiter of human reality, it was a natural next step for me to move the locus of resonance from the Chair itself to take as the *thing*, another poem, an event, a loss, a contradiction or a combination of these in order to evade Rilke's strict terrain of the thing itself and move toward territories of my own while keeping the Chair in a precise focus.

In this way, it became possible to use the Chair for engagement on my own terms, exploring my own modes of discourse and observation. This serves as a kind of braiding of concerns that includes the dignified Chair that surfaces from time to time in philosophy, the gesture toward Rilke's refinements, and a weaving of certain relevancies into poems of my own.

The paintings of Gloria Matuszewski have provided a stability of momentum that has answered the call to create out of air, out of will, through a certain purposefulness that attaches to nothing, needs nothing, asks for nothing, is, perhaps, nothing. And she and I have turned all of that nothing into something. Gloria would put all this differently perhaps, but her will *to make* is greater than anything she or I may say about process or motive. I followed her as she went.

In this sense, *The Chairs* becomes the place where creativity, that wonder of commitment and purposefulness, derives from the breath, seeking only appreciation in answer.

And that is why this book is dedicated to Peter Graasbol Schmidt, the Great Appreciator and my Beloved Husband, whose patience and support are limitless in space.

NMH
New York City
August 2022

DEDICATIONS & ACKNOWLEDGMENTS

from the Painter

THESE paintings are dedicated to my daughter Jessica Lee Molligan and my grandson Miles Michael Molligan Scott, to my daughter Liza Jane Molligan DeMartini and son-in-law Paul Edward DeMartini and my grandson Jack Edward DeMartini, and to the memory of Patricia C. Kearns whose San Francisco flat mirrored my childhood flat and wherein I could be "home" when need be, and to Brian Allen Beveridge, for being at my side for most of this work, and to my sister, Louise Marie Mattis Lutz. And, as always, to the memory of my parents, Susan Pereksta Mattis and Louis Stanley Mattis (also known as Louis Stanley Matuszewski).

I also wish to acknowledge the following who have been not unlike my favorite Chair, comforting, steadfast, supportive in grand ways and in countless seemingly insignificant moments. A few have passed but their presence forever lingers.

With deep appreciation to Barbara Alderson, Lori Austin, Michael Ellis Banister, Bradford C. Bennett, Ann Bernauer, Andrew Lowman Beveridge, Virginia Louise Snyder Beveridge, Nancy Sidney Brinn, Kathleen Brown, Natica Yates Cecchetti, Ronald Collins, Mary Coyne, Roy De Gorog, Sheila Molligan Diecidue, Christine Durbin, Barbara Dwyer, Wanda Ford, Kamala Friedman, Carolyn M. Garvin, Christopher Gentry, William Calvin Hammett, Judy Lee Henderson, Skip Henderson, Patrick Johnson, Yofe Johnson, Kathleen Lack, Nicole Lutz Laris, Gene Lieberman,

Kerin Lieberman, Kate McCracken, Norma J. McKeldin-Barnett, Maria Medua, Melanie Wendt Molligan, Michael Molligan, Peter Nicholas Molligan, Rene Juliette Molligan, Violet Augusta Scheeler Molligan, Haruko Mukasa, Nancy Ann Murray, Andra Norris, Michele Nye, Susan Ann Olson, Nancy Perkins, Nora Privitera, David Williams Rising, Daniel Rising, Melinda Rising, Glen Rogers, Suzanne Roth, Danielle Rowan, Betsy Russell, Peter Graasbol Schmidt, Sparkie Spaeth, Barbara Stanley, Laurie Thompson, Gaia Toscano, Doug Wilson, Angela Wood, Betty Wood and Carol Mihalik Yates.

GM
Novato, California
August 2022

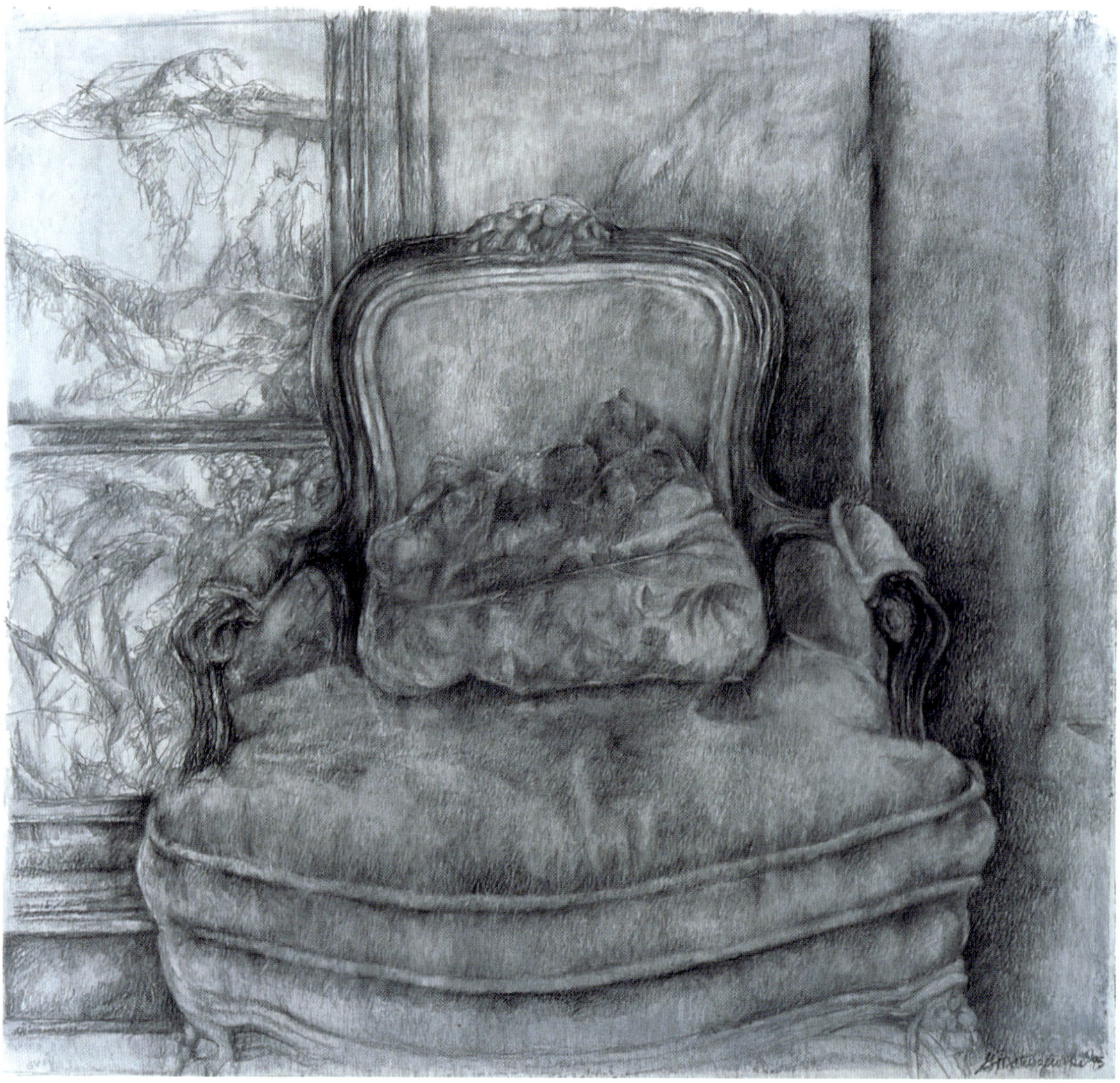

I

We abandon ourselves into your empty
arms, chair, turning our faces to the wall.
In a reverie of peace, we collapse
against the sinking pillows of your frame.

What hand has closed the window
at your side and backed you here
into this corner of despair? Is it time
to turn and face the precipice outside?

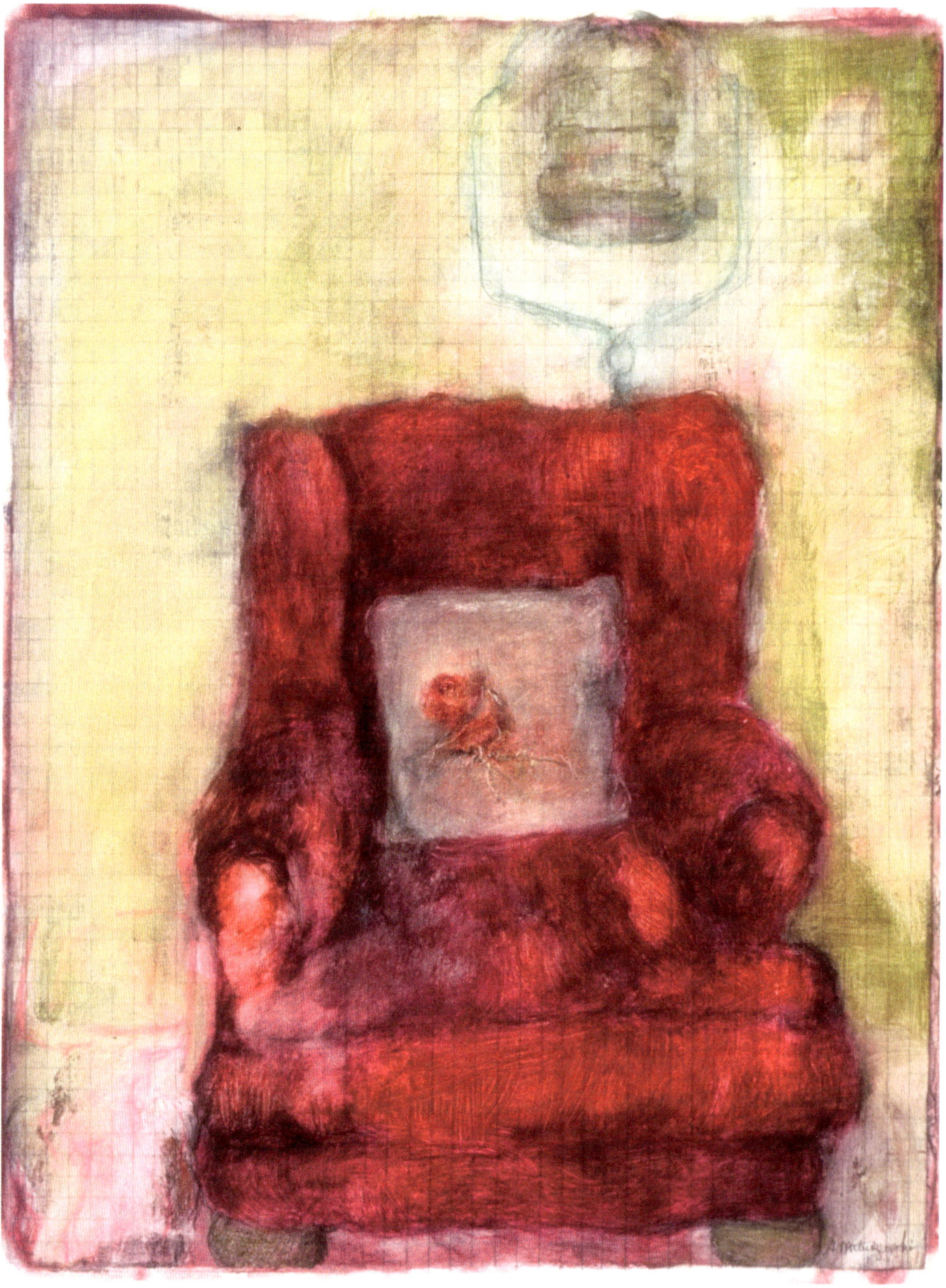

II

The emptiness of which you know
the secret, chair, arrests us as we
burst by you dreaming in the hall.
You reminisce at leisure,

unperturbed at how our pace
precludes our sitting down. Yet,
often, in the seams of twilight,
your glance shatters every thought.

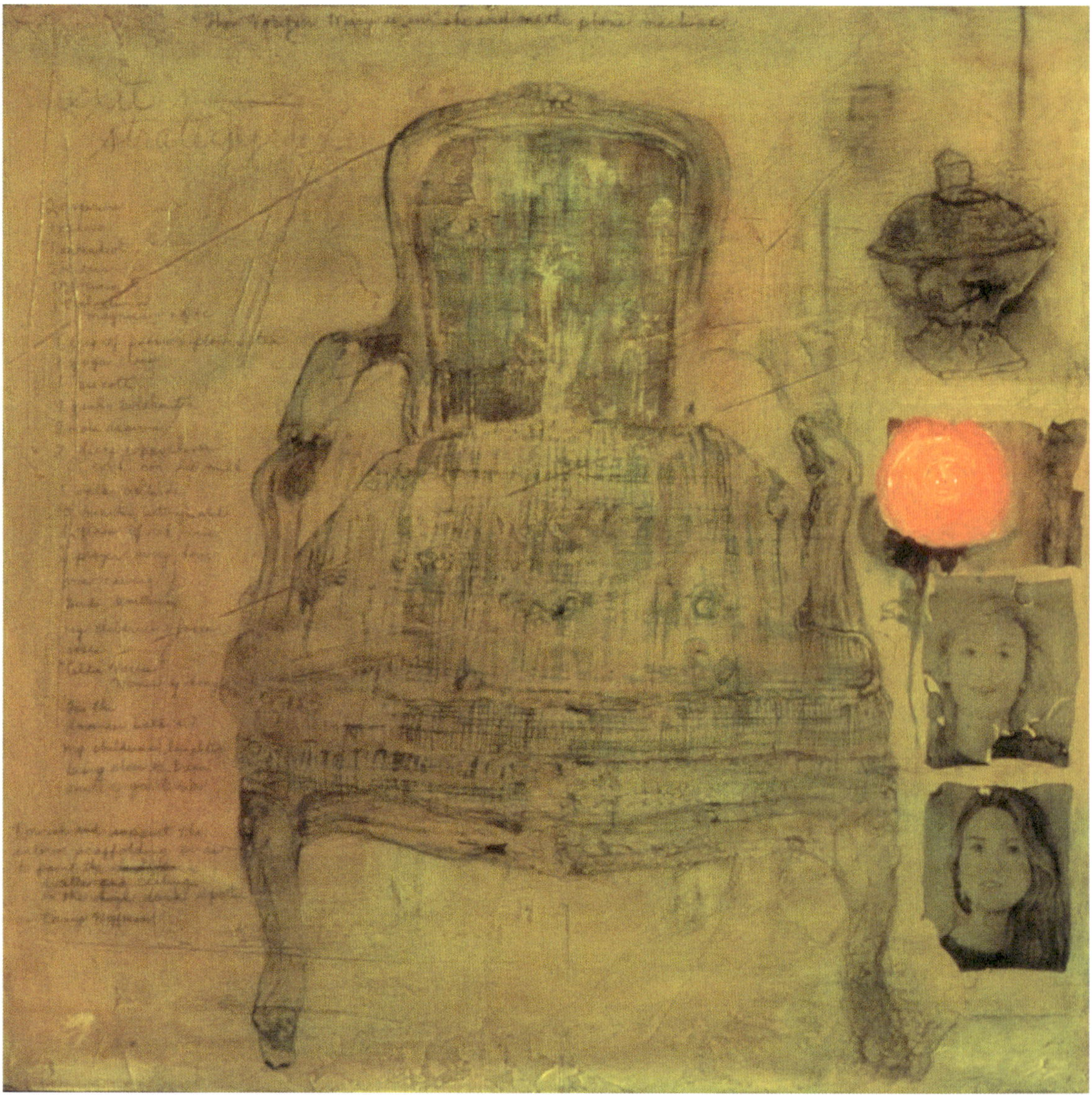

III

In a private moment, chair,
I take you by the arm.
It is as if, in this window light,
the first idea were born.

How many sudden companions
have found you in this repose,
where your relaxed attention
vanishes in reflection?

How many ardent thinkers
sat and dreamed? Dreamed
and, dreaming, settled here
more deeply, as you sighed.

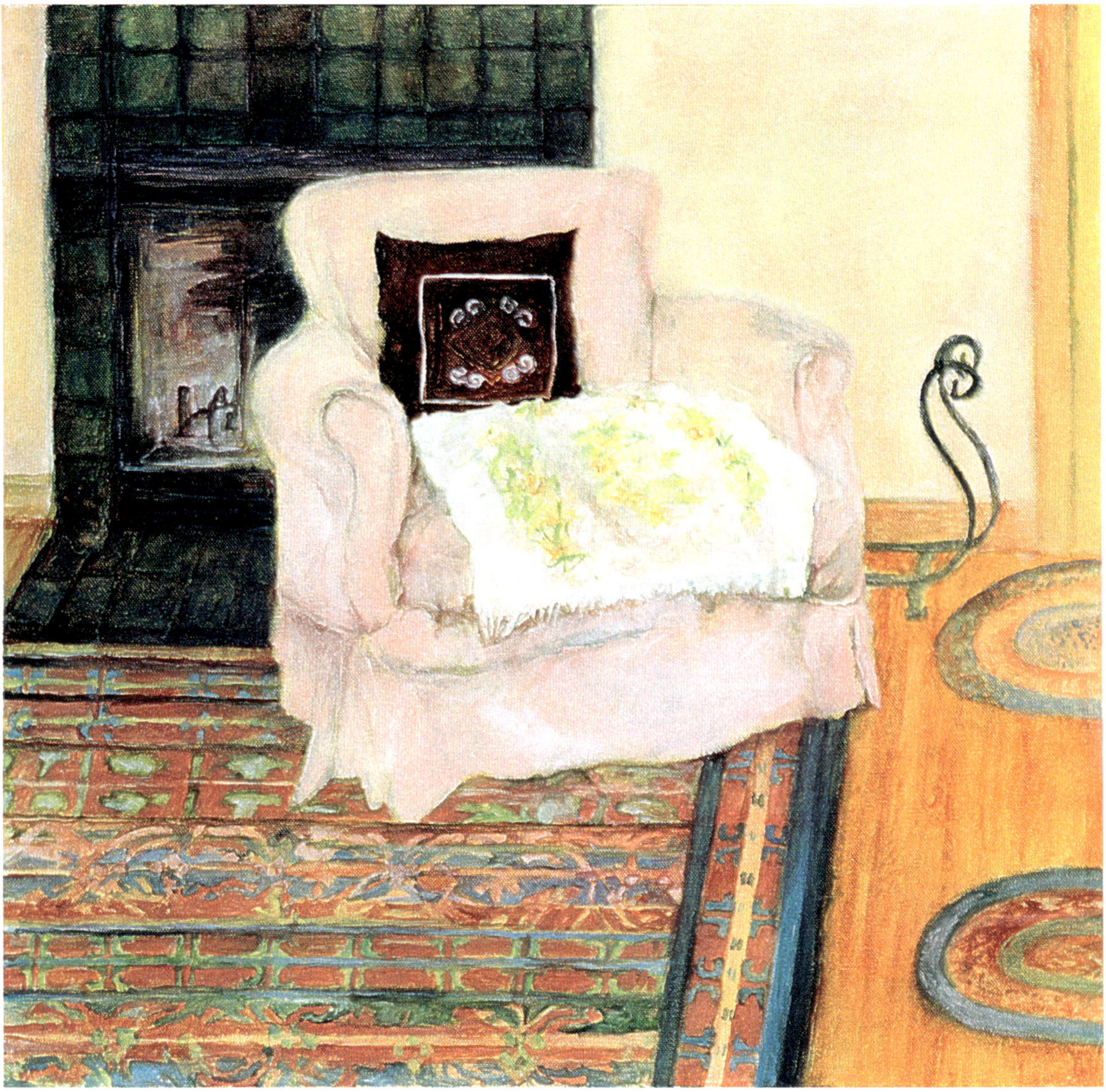

IV

Springtime: to sit down
where you beckon,
just as the breath of the air
frisks into the room.

I rest my cheek
against your grey velour,
companionable friend,
after rain. You creak,
but say nothing of how
you passed the night.

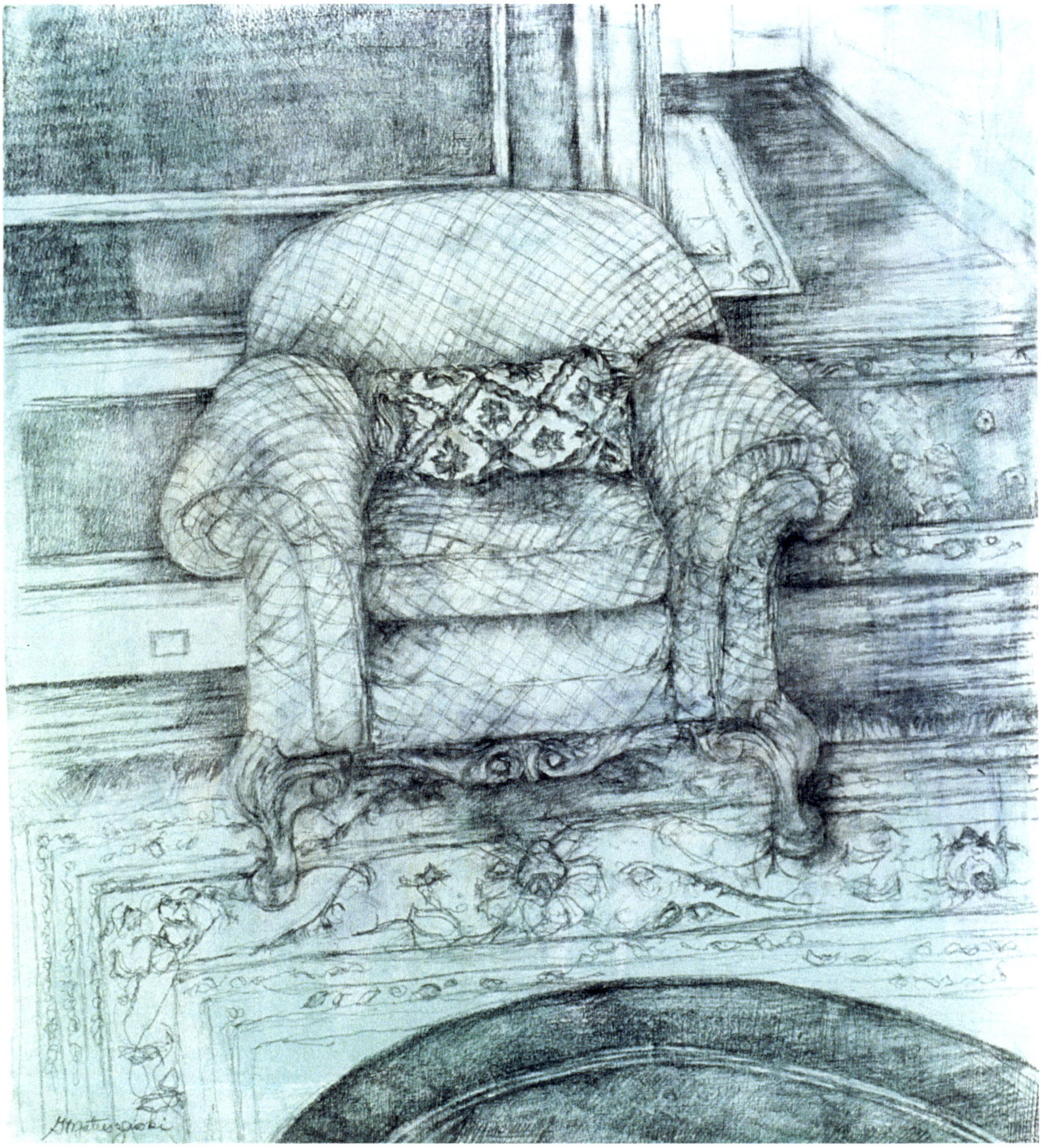

V

To be welcomed into your
exuberant, waiting self –
had I been an hour early,
you might be bearing
fruits or folded clothes.

I have found you, not in disarray,
but ready. You lean back
voluptuously and I rejoice
to find you free!

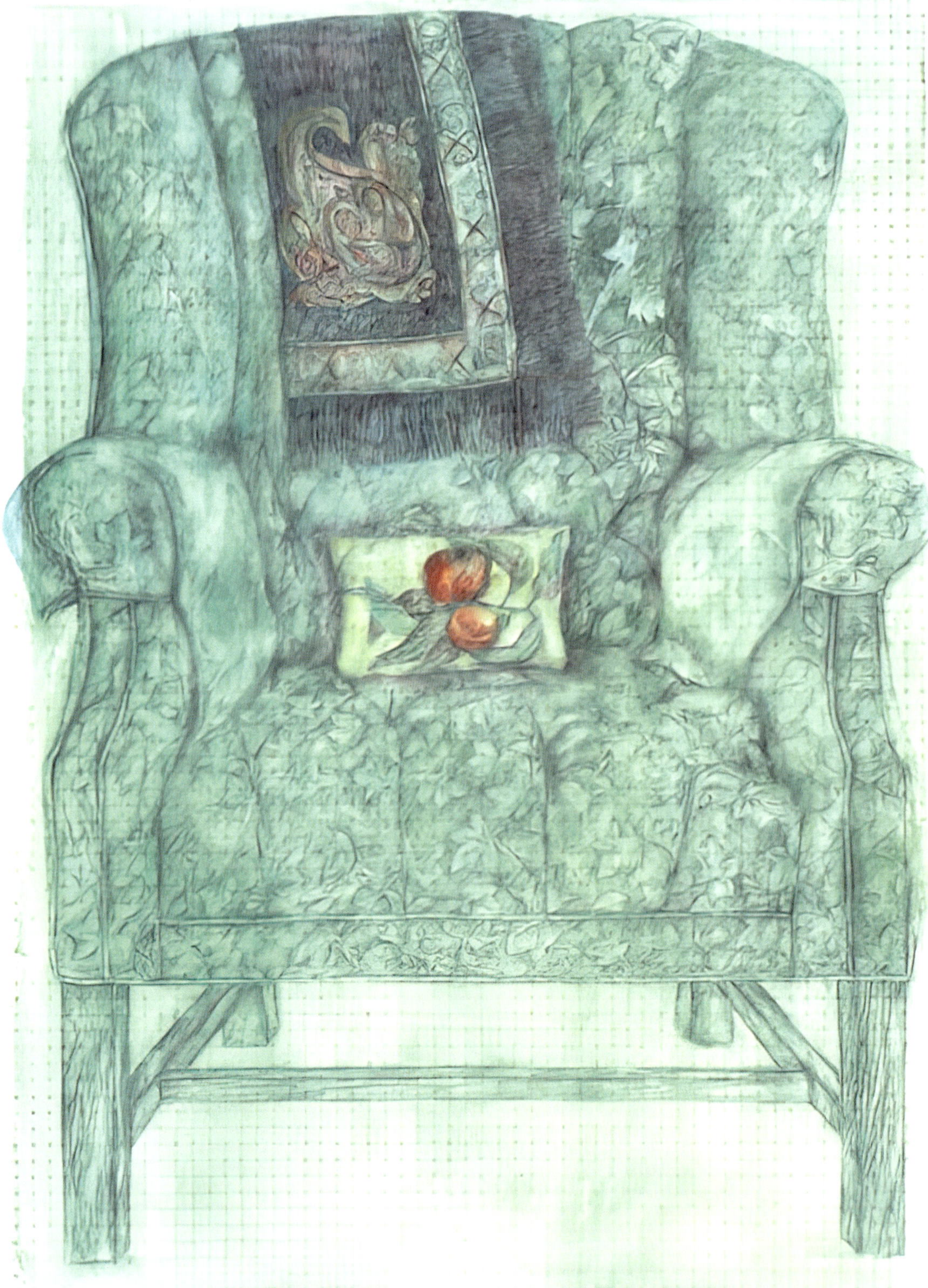

VI

Is it too terrible just
to sit here, with you, all alone –
where you, without judgment,
require nothing to be done?

To be a chair completely naked
in the hall. To rest, perhaps
bestrewn with an exotic throw.
To do nothing at all, all day long.

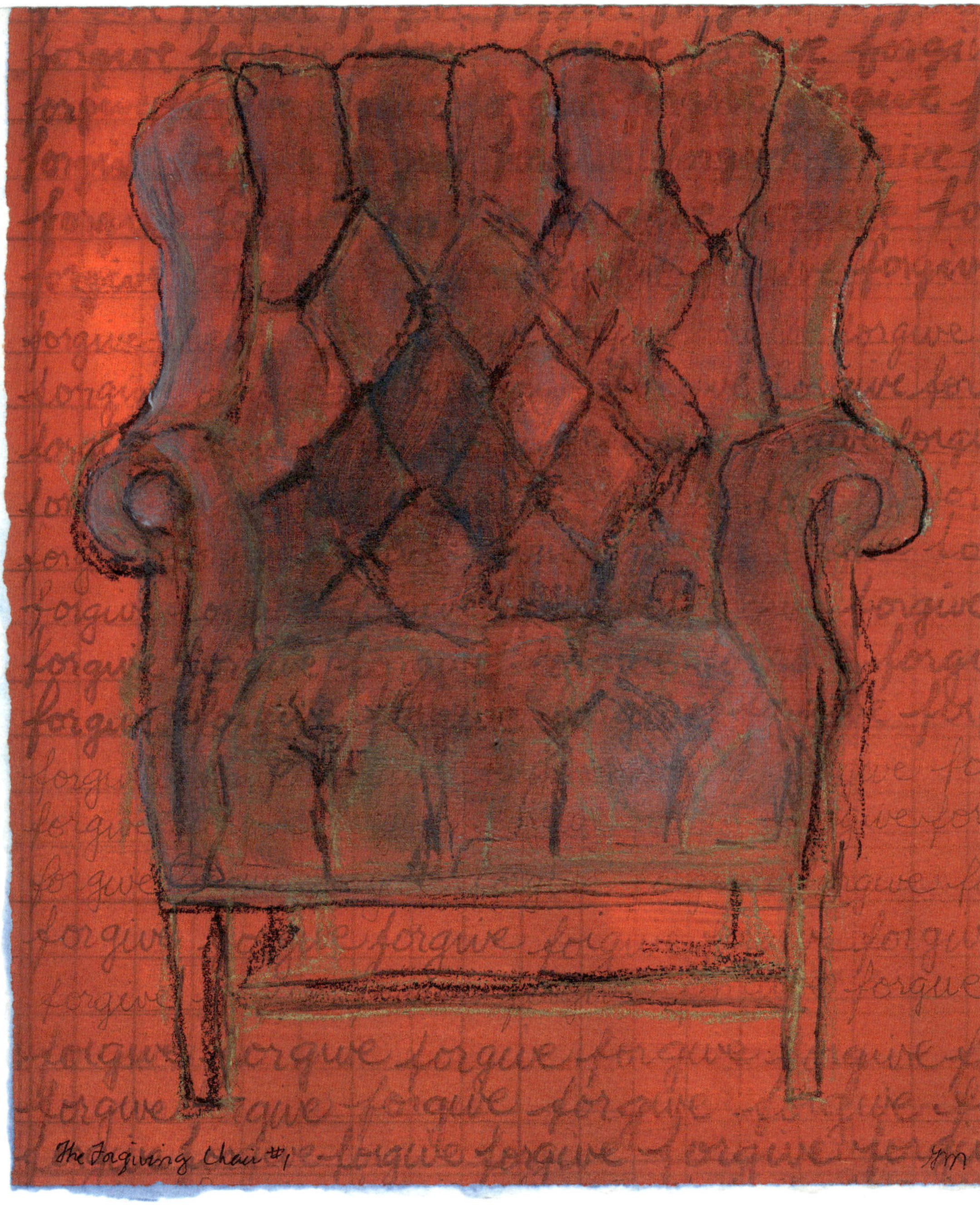
The Forgiving Chair #1

VII

Sometimes they die in you,
that famous electric moment.
You are impassive at restraint,
impervious to shock.

Centered in the staging ground,
you acquiesce. It is another
mother's child in your lap.
You simply steel your gaze,
and face down the crowd.

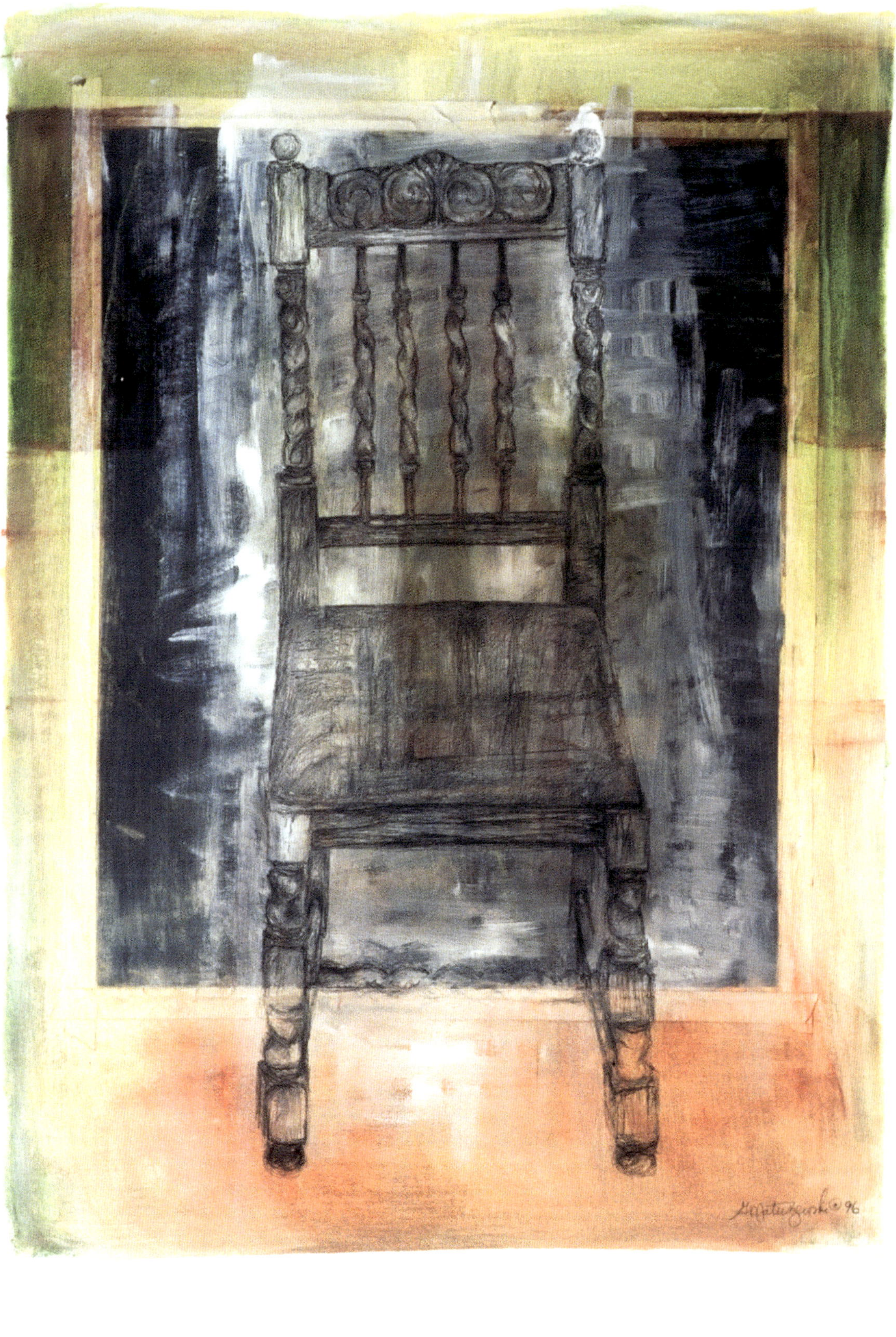

VIII

To be ensconced in an ornate chair.
To be aware of the wooden
uncials carved behind, beside,
below. What a carver
might do to embellish you!

Chair of the remarkable gesture!
Chair wrought and brought to gleam,
to glow. Wooden, stable, genuine –
two bare hands grip you
to make you, and, later,
grip you to wait.

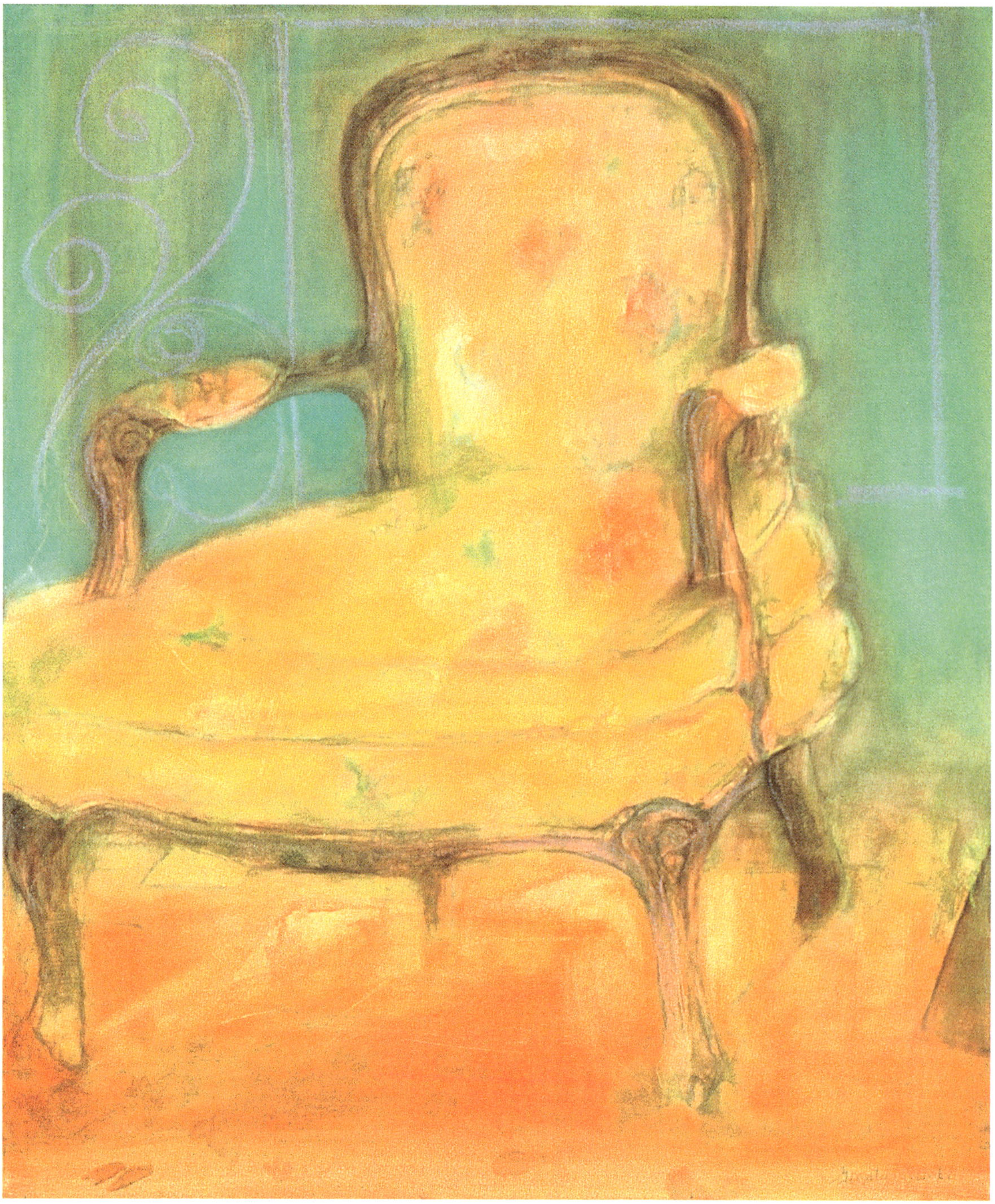

IX

In you resides the rest
that exists inside motion,
the poise of a man just
at the head of a stair.

Your stillness, chair,
is as certain as desire,
or longing before descent to grief
or love before the rush of joy.

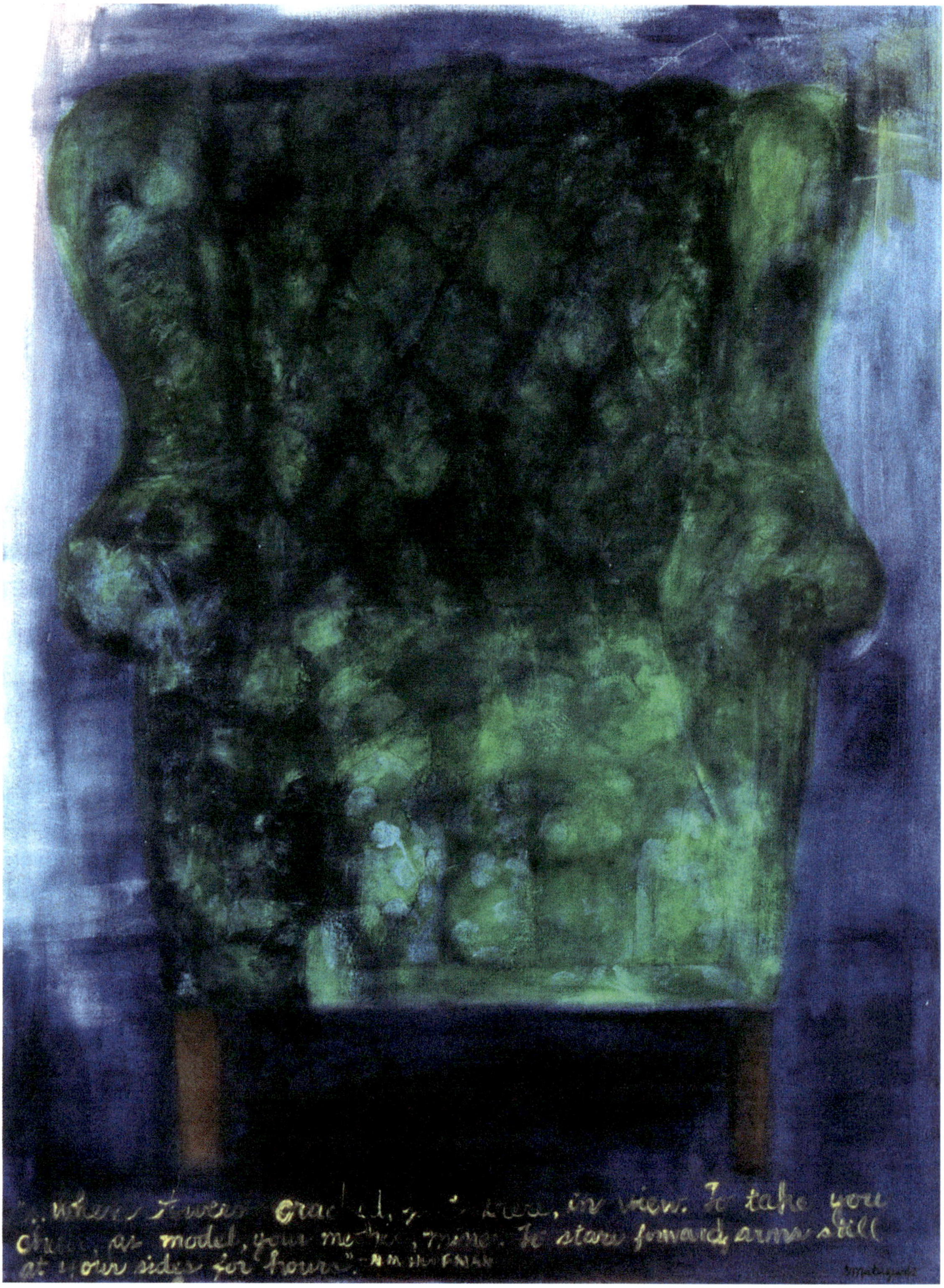
in view. To take you
as model, your mother, mine. To stare forward, arms still
at your sides for hours."

X

No one had a better mentor,
in shock of smoke, in tragedy
or attack. To be taught,
to take the lesson in, when towers

cracked, just there, in view.
To take you, chair, as model,
your method, mine. To stare forward,
arms still at your sides for hours.

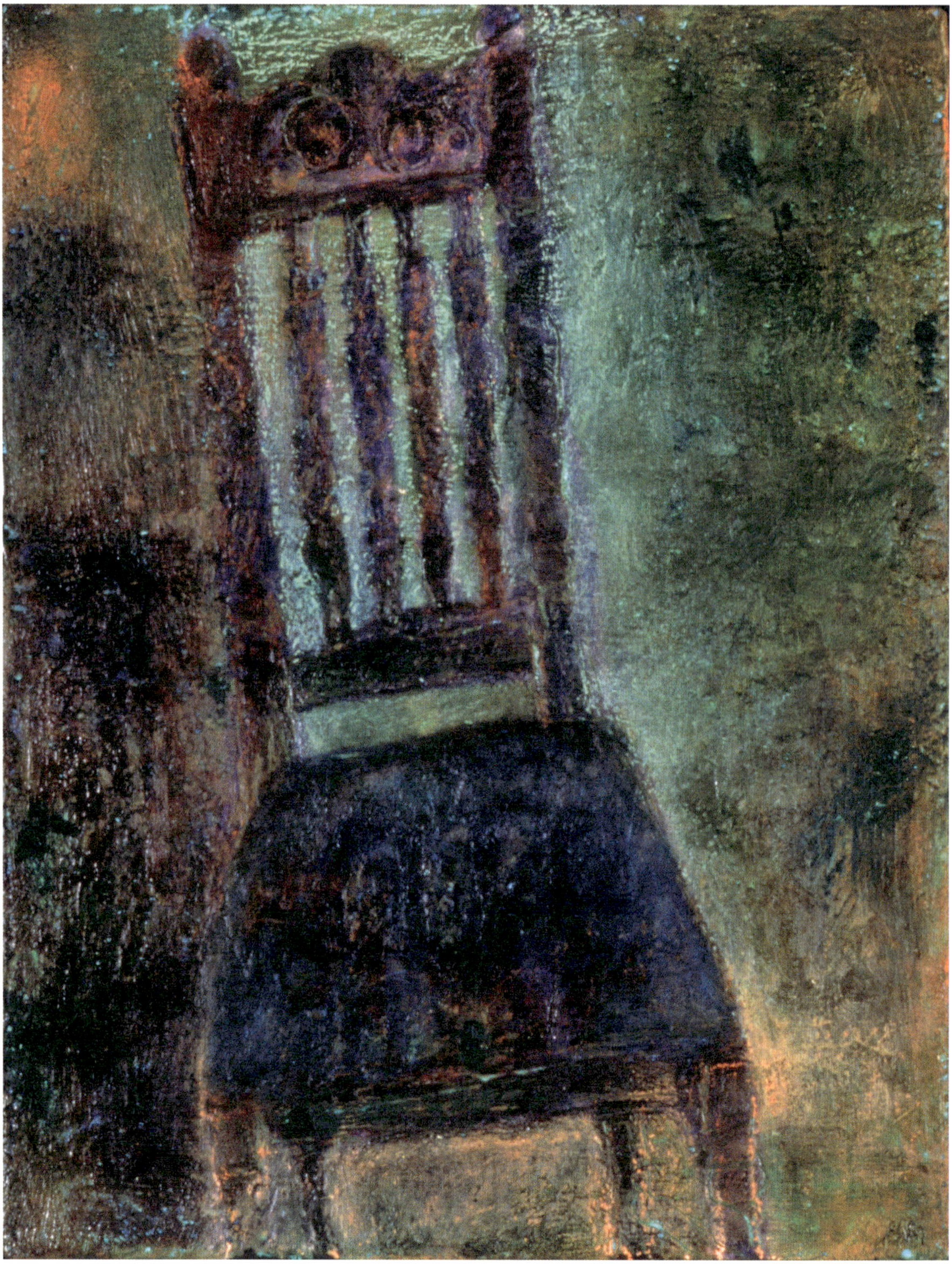

XI

You are a rune on the slate slab
at the foot of the steep stair
in a blazing sun. Beside you,
the white root of wild horseradish
glistens where it has been cut.

Grandmother after grandmother
stoops to you, leaning back
against the hot brick wall.

If we scrape away the sea green paint,
beneath the grime of vegetable stain,
hidden is the foreign uncial "M" –
Mutter, müssen, Mädchen, Mutter.

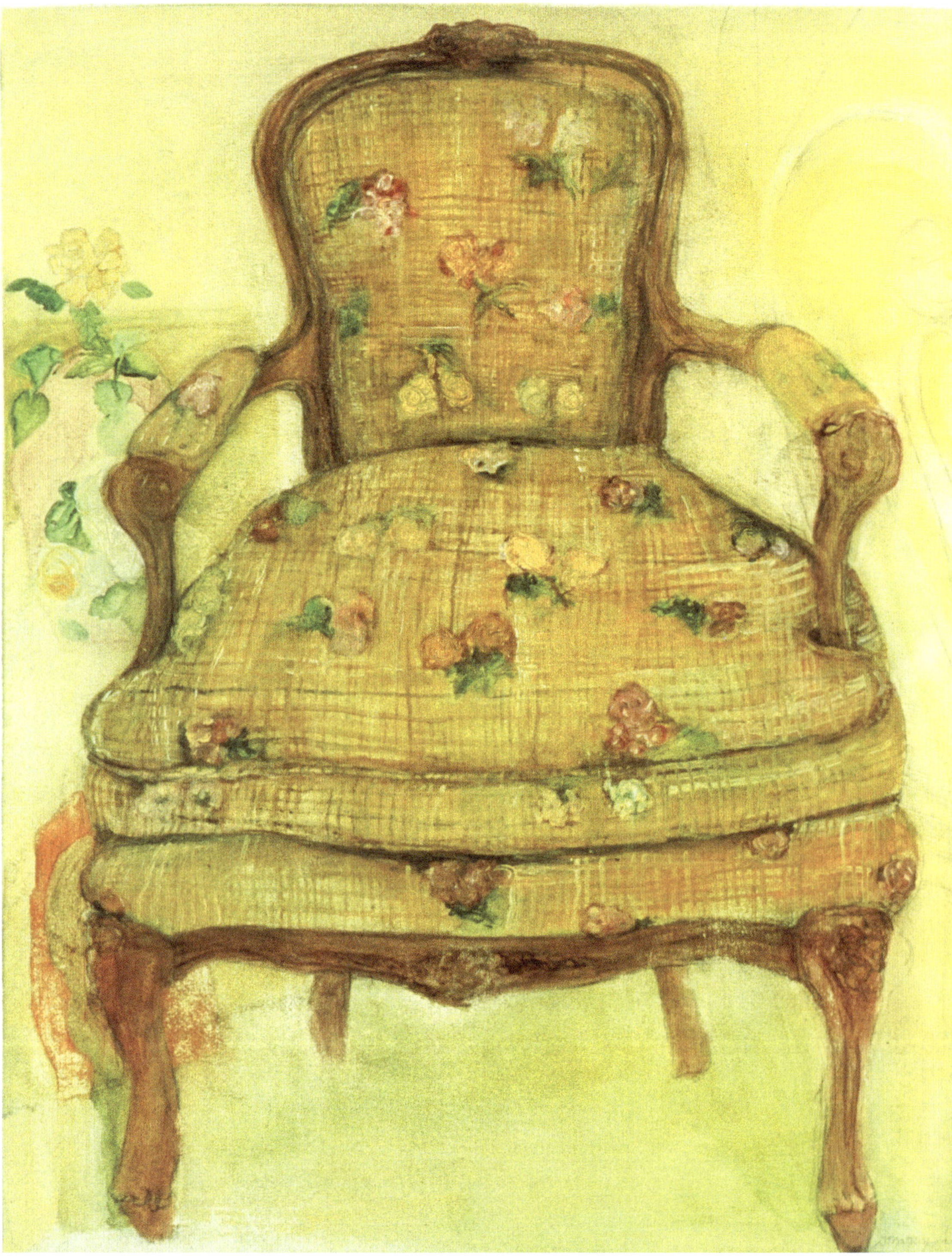

XII

When a hand flutters to rest
on your arm and the occasion requires
dignity, the certainty of foundations,
concrete assessment, sovereign
assumption of complete control,
you, chair, alone, keep it all
from crashing to the floor.

Plinth to the person, the place
where, stolid locus of intention,
the sitter grasps the scepter
of the self, surveys the eyes' estate,
and settles in your throne of charm.

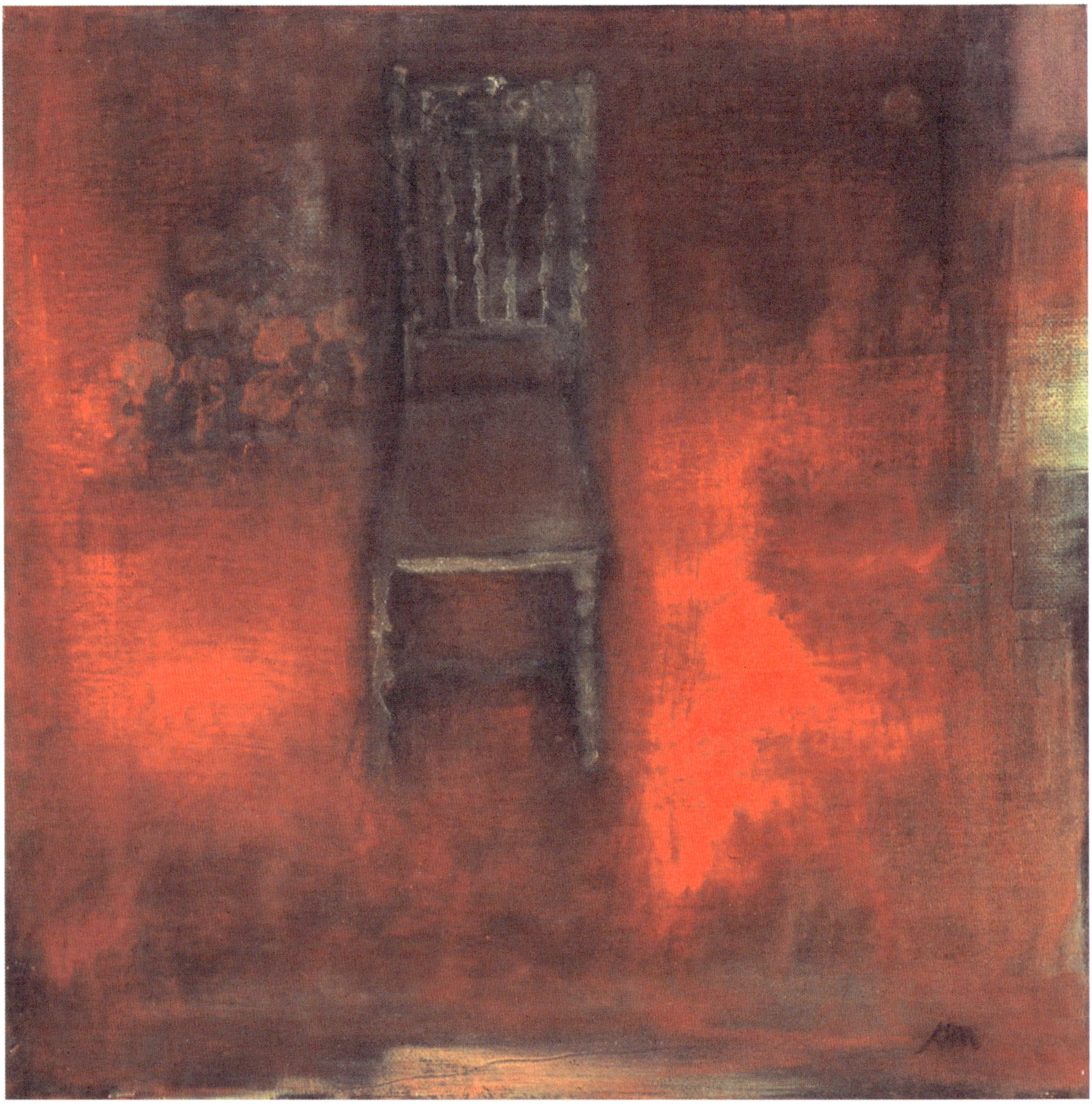

XIII

We live seated in a tall chair, so high
our feet no longer touch the ground.

Chair, you hear the name of a Texan, born
in Maine, a maniac, in half-conversations,
and see his worm's fingers jabbing in air.
You are dumbfounded at so many loaded words.

Shiny black boots rest on your rungs,
but Nobody seems to be there.
Yet he is so close to you had he a moustache,
you would see the cockroaches darting in and out.

Meantime half-human underlings fling new laws
like horseshoes against your legs.
Are they authorized? They of whom
the hollow skull never has known so much?

Nobody made the laws and Nobody broke them.
A corpulent hand rests along your back
and the twenty years go by.

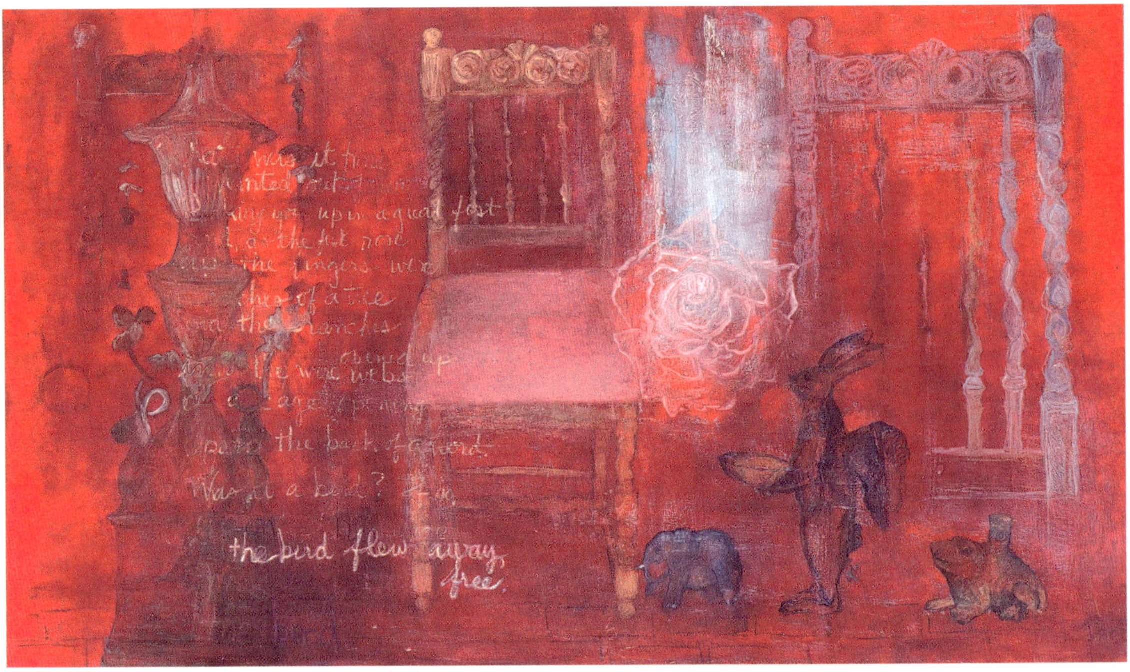
the bird flew away,
free.

XIV

I am ancient and my mind is
above giving the lie to body's torpor.

If I break a chair over the head of memory,
does the mind wake to clearer memory?
or does the memory die? or does
the mind die as it is remembering?

If I remember a wall, a tower,
which they built to pen me in,
what is it to build a wall much later
to pen them out? Is this the great
labyrinth of another's being?

I will imagine a memory that burns
its way into forgetfulness, like a kind
of dawn in which the sun burns a hole
in the mist, scalding the horizon
to perfected vision as pieces
of the chair clatter to the ground.

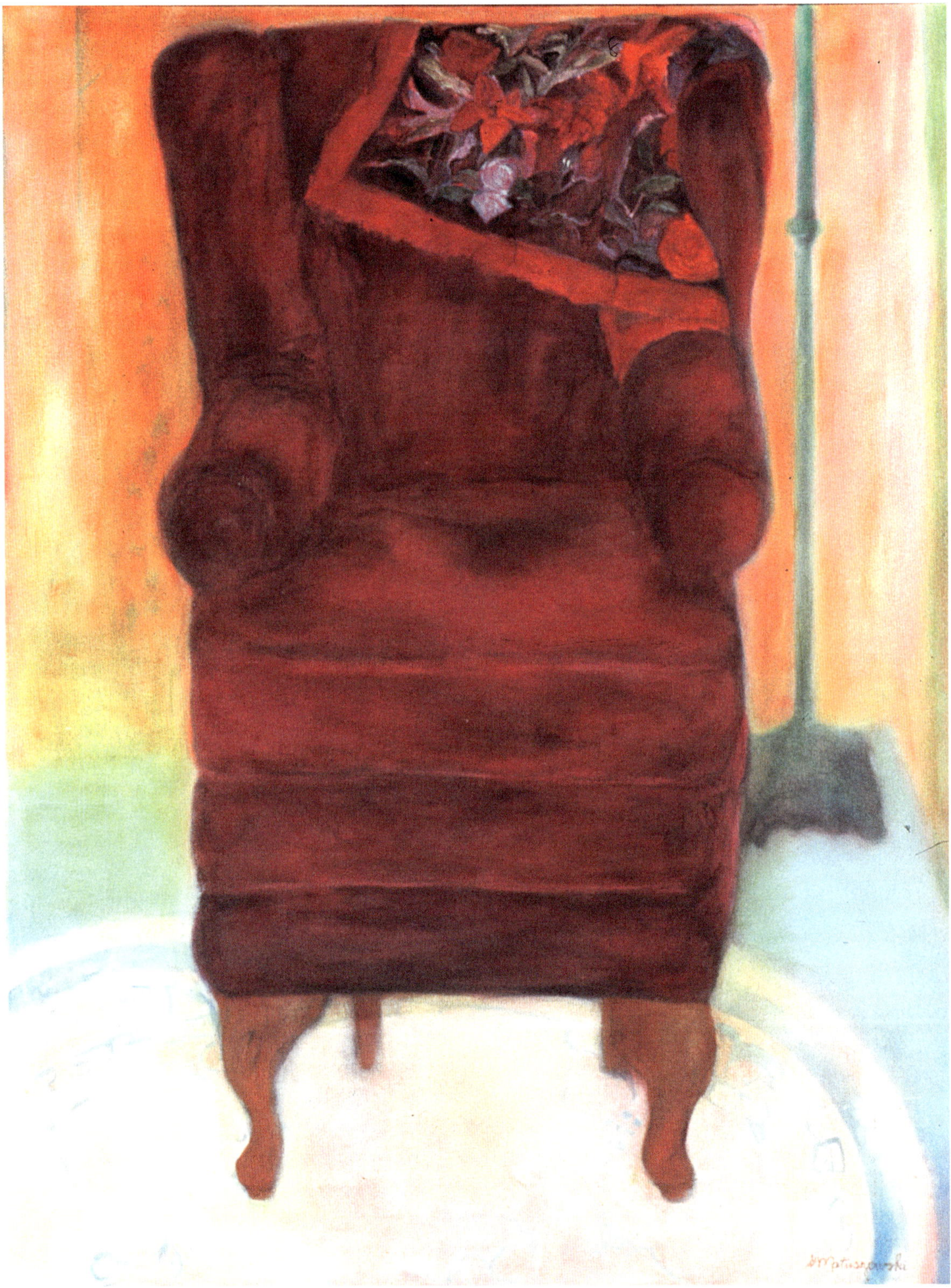

XV

Seasons of war, to him in his deep chair,
braid into family matters, musterings, marriages –
the old sameness of dramatic pasts.

Antimacassars of primordial battles
slope into this revered elder's post-Bulge opening
of a death camp, his witnessings in later years.

And as he fought through Germany, his younger
brother, Robert, was blown up by accident in
a Luxembourg mine field. He shrugged.
"What are you going to do?"

War, then, a weather beneath a bronze star,
piercing of wind, weight of snow, deep
chair, empty now, with where he had to go.

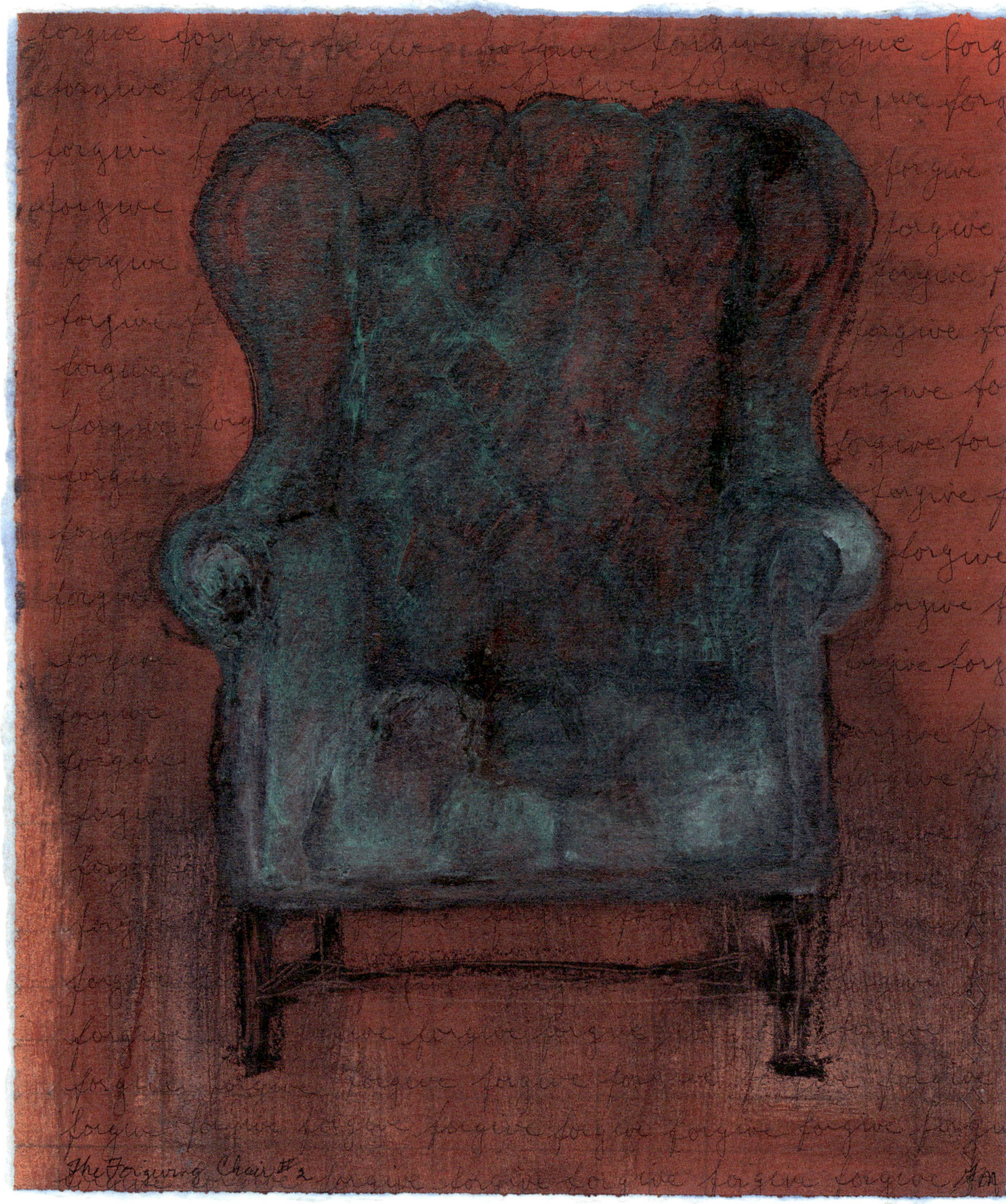
The Forgiving Chair #2

XVI

Something physical usually does motivate
the vastest resource. Butterfly wings
cough the gentle billow tending to tsunami.

An idea of the end of borders continues
on, similarly billowing, through wire, through
artificial wall and bulwark, through cracked
and bitter mental stasis, through loping Time.

You can taste it in your chair at river edge:
the light, a garment, and the heavens like a tent.

The "yes" you say to seat yourself draws
a second chair out of the shadow. The day
moon marks the season. Yes says "yes"
to yes and the Great Yes sits at last
down in the chair of peace.

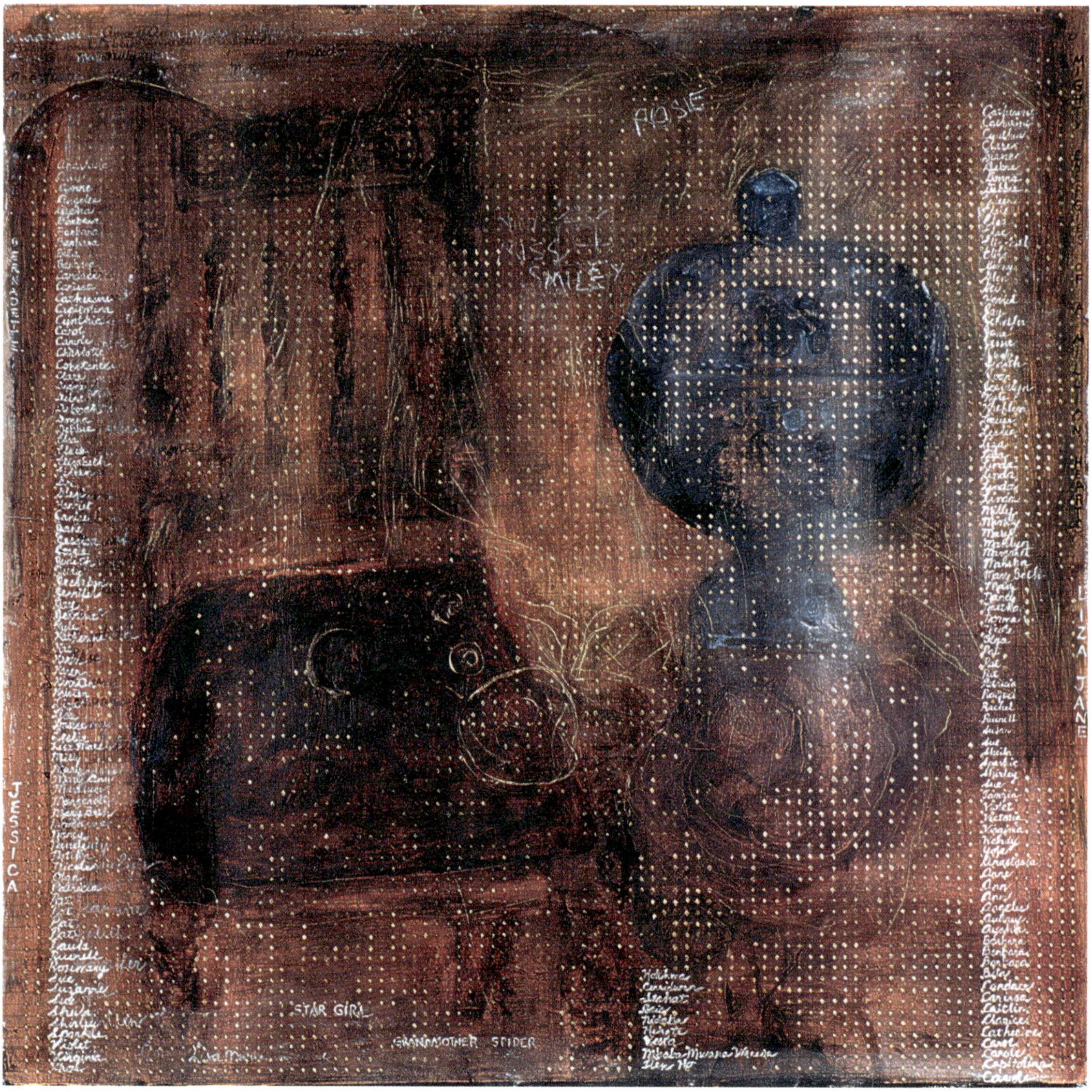
ROSE
SMILEY
STAR GIRL
GRANDMOTHER SPIDER
JESSICA
LIZA JANE

XVII

Simply a mobilized seat, no sedan chair
for pasha, not anything but a running
board's companion in the crowd.

Back seat for her, you are famed for framing
wars. Would you have preferred to stack
up with spindly others, just alike to you?

You would have missed Calliope come
sweeping at you in her catastrophic
fireball and merely rested arm in arm
with compeers, rigid, on the palace floor.

Glory to burn for the people, smell of burnt
leather, smoke still pouring from your springs,
under which she had tucked her golden shoes.

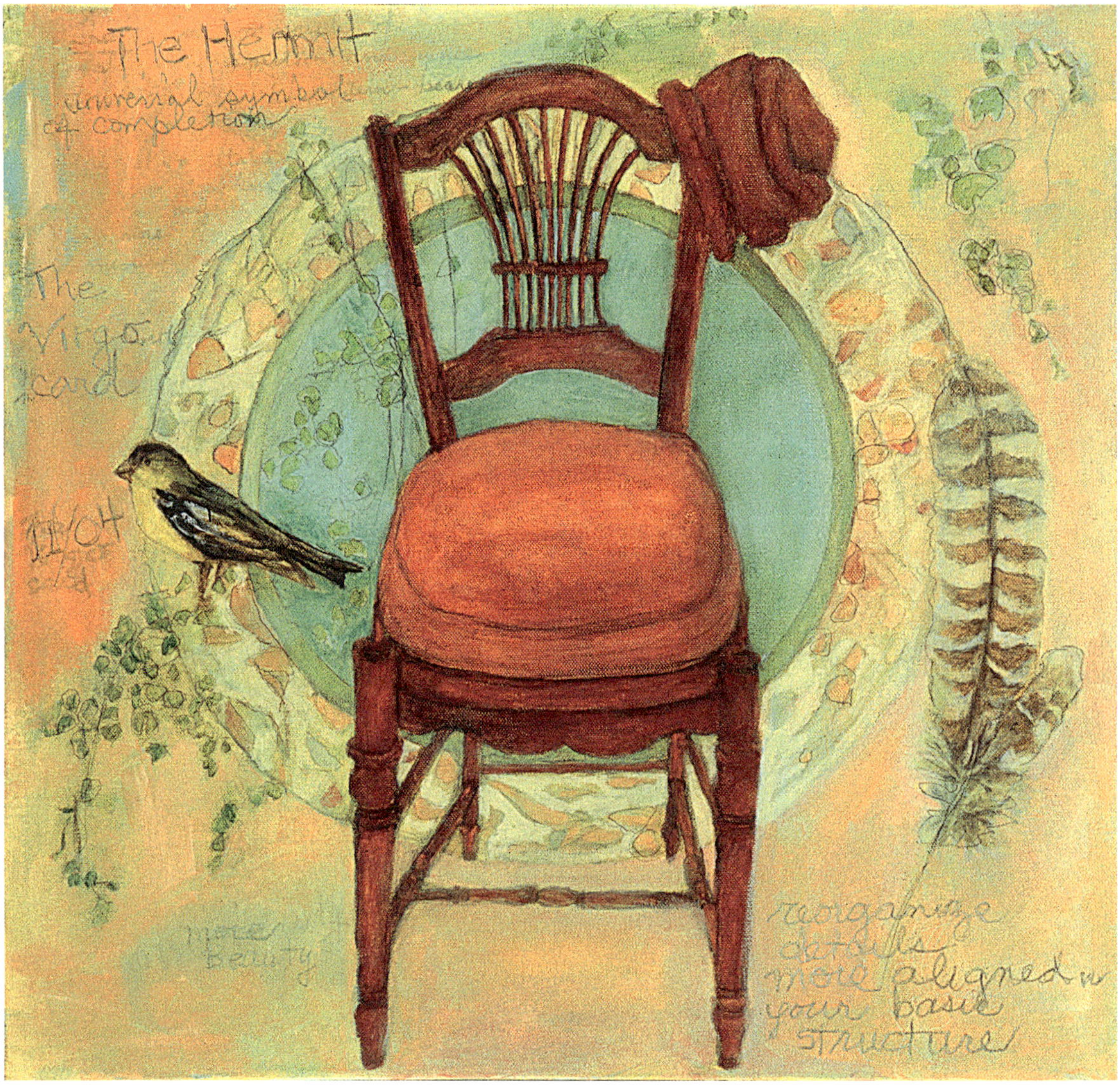
The Hermit
universal symbol
of completion
The
Virgo
card
11/04
more
beauty
reorganize
details
more aligned w
your basic
structure

XVIII

May I take your beguiled flows,
lift you from that ashen urn.

Shall I shape you as the master
with the clay between the fingers,
squeezing. No, a chair, see –
Hamada's chair collection.

Let that be what is to me
the shape perfected, to hold up
to the light is all, to view
with keen appreciation, what
the place is from where to see.

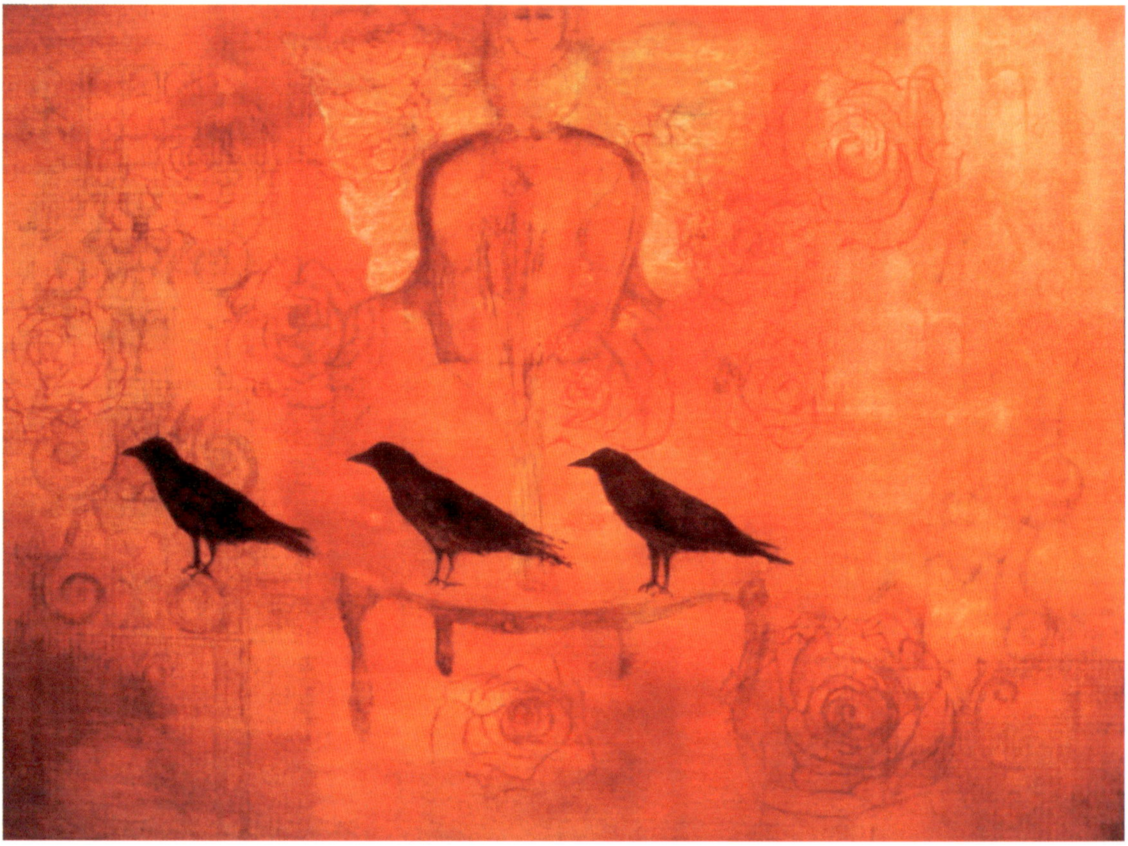

XIX

Anchoring the long hall – what
you did in the deep night –
swiveling between the street
and reception.

Emergencies navigated and the viral
new kind, there as you made place
between the world in front
and that behind.

Tableau of care: we shipwrecked
in plague and you swiveled for
those sentries at the door, before any
thought of parade.

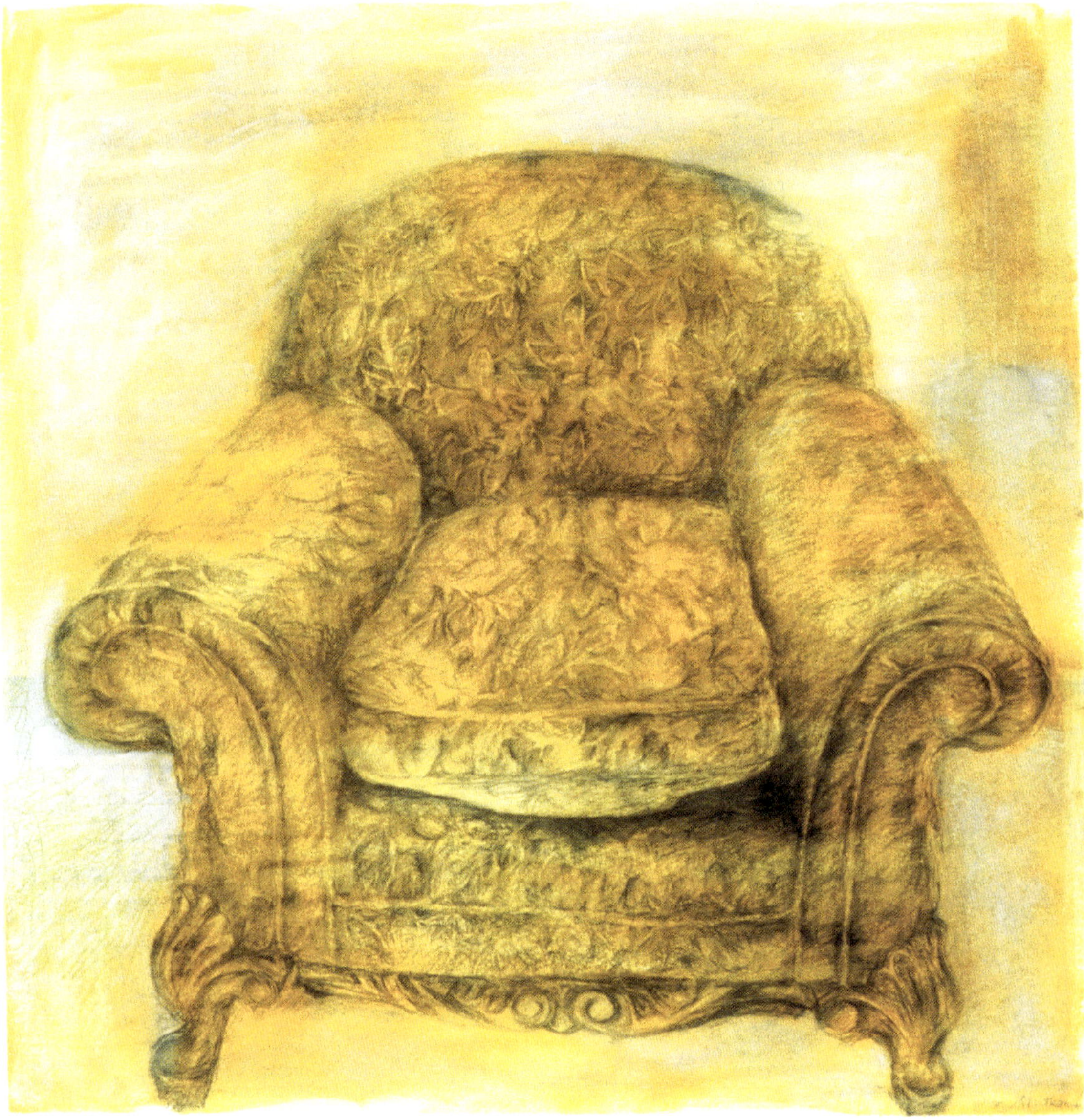

XX

A velvet rope across your lap
where no one sits except perhaps
as placeholder in mind, no more
to do with our affairs than
last years' clouds. We tender
names, but not for shepherds now.

Our madness is like ocean
and we cannot lance our hurts.

We see the place where comfort sat
without compunction, lost to change,
and you, unchanging, are not for us,
but remind us of that seat we lost.

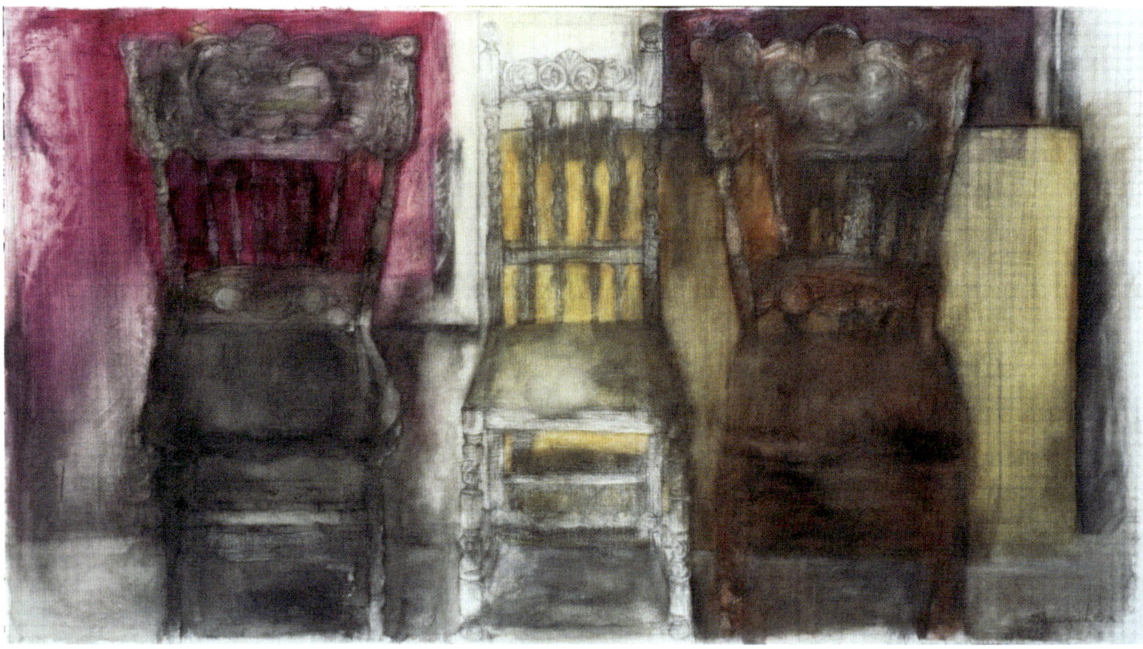

XXI

It was a secret ministry facing off
with enablers, demanding passports,
creating anguish instead of borderlessness.
They continue to sit withdrawn from the world
while you, chairs, stiffen with each one's weight.

Children removed from their parents
by some supposing themselves just.
Children killed outright as "collateral
damage," while, withdrawn, the rest
pretend to lawfulness and humanity.

Where some have sat invoking violence,
the rest have sat in silent frost,
witness to your creaking and collapse,
in face of steady cruelty and lies.

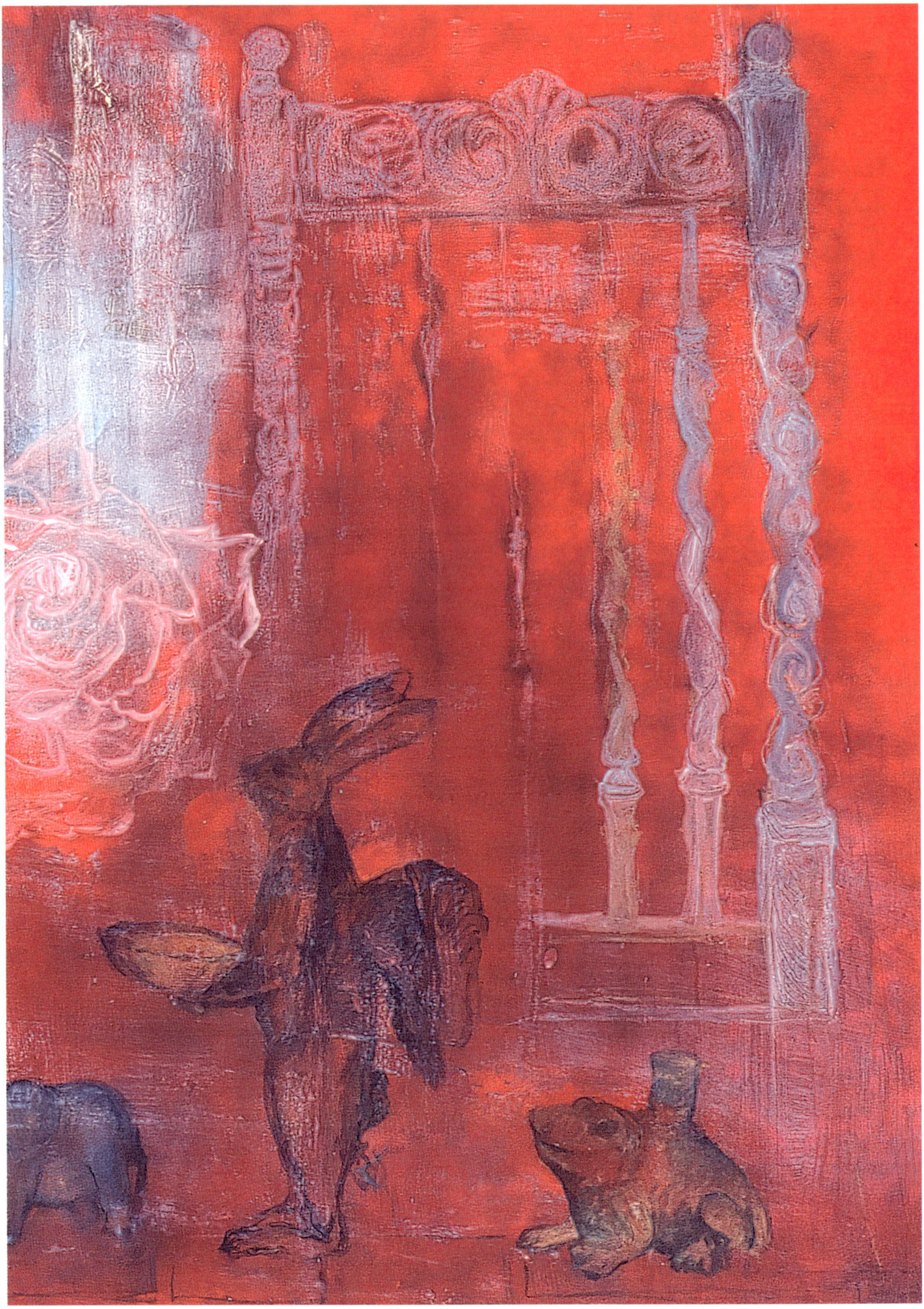

XXII

Those wheels support your mercy
as you support the old, the frail.
In back, a pack for lunch,
umbrellas, a radio, a phone.

It is true, you are pushed
and you cooperate, moving
forward as the time requires.
A pony ride with owls and moon?

Perhaps. What you have rivaled
in the way of bones, of maturations,
can you, seat with wheels, renounce
the next mock response to pain.

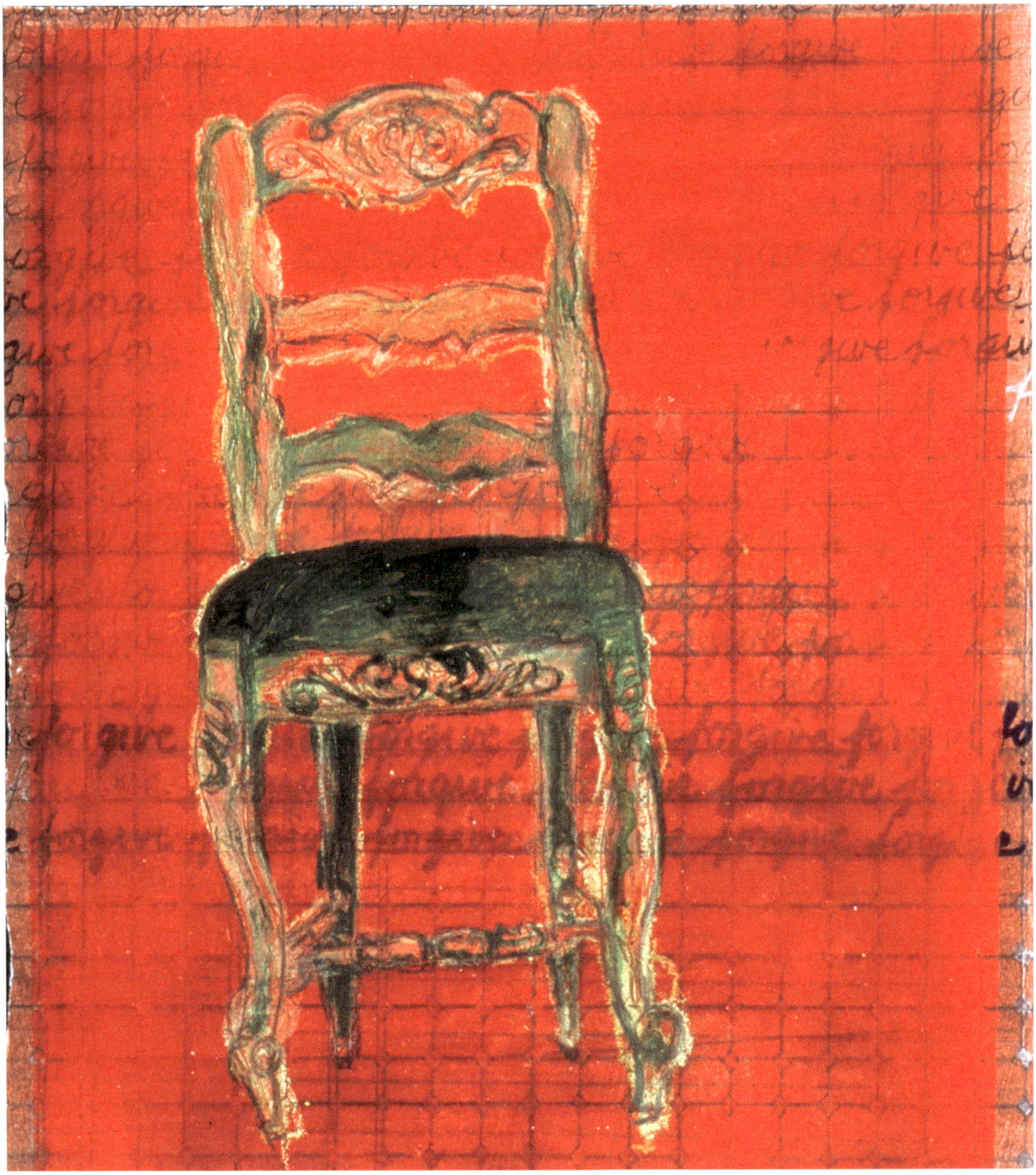

XXIII

Others may win as races go,
Reaching out for palm and gold,
Kipchoge will not rest we know
Out of frailty or failure of will.

In him the Nandi resistance sits,
Yesterday's wisdom and prophecy,
Operative now in this flying man,
The new seat of special powers.

Electric racer, visionary as to purpose.
Lead us to that reason to fly on,
Innovative, indomitable in spirit realms.
Usher us to be spirit seats ourselves,
Determined in the clear space ahead.

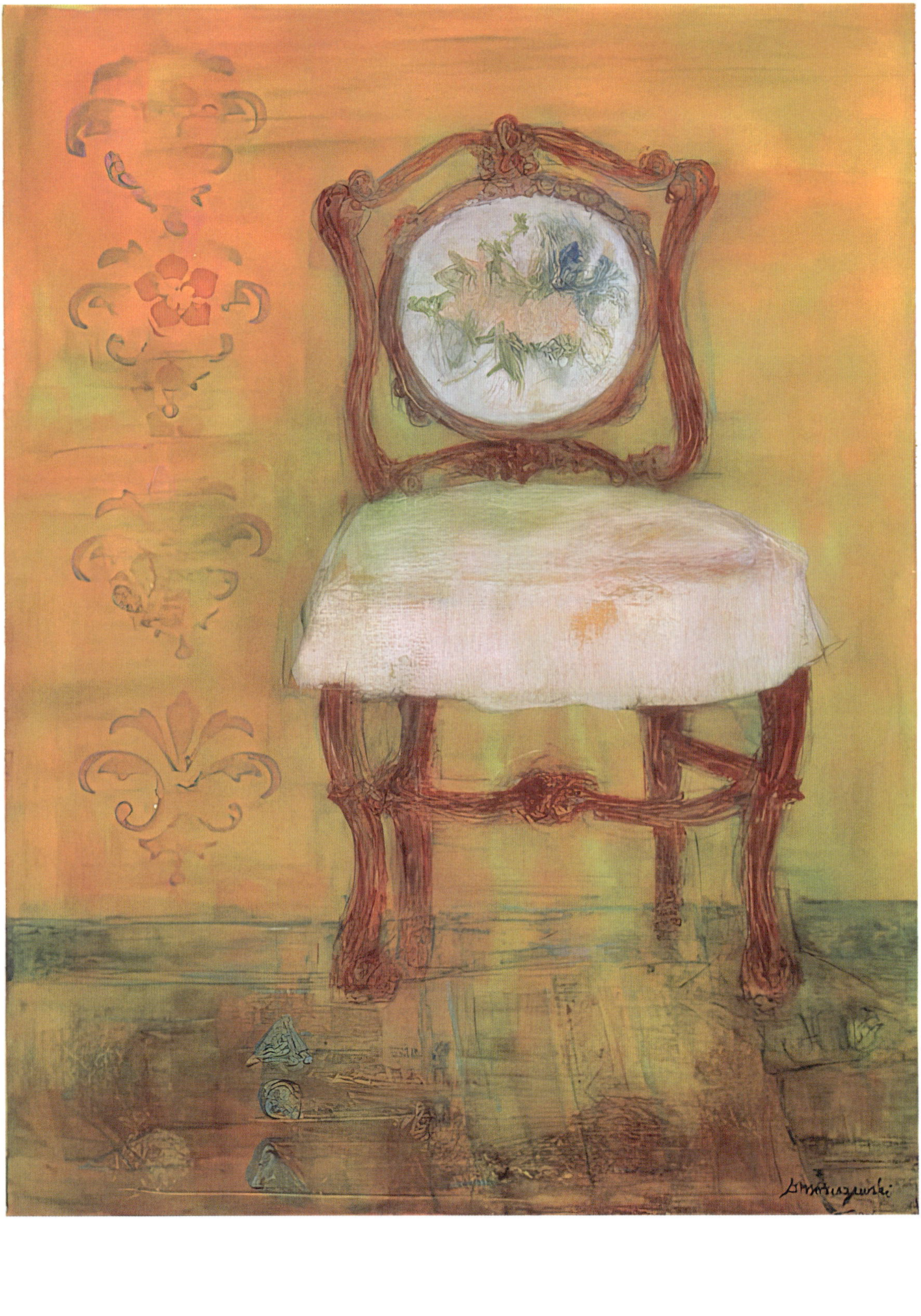

XXIV

At the wheel, feet press out elemental
rhythm, legs join with hip, with back,
with mirth; round wheel and round seat –
the round way toward power.

Energy to bring the power round –
the salt-glazed bellarmine where
granite decomposes and sets free feldspar
of its alkaline, sweet clay leading,
resisting heat, achieving that moment's color.

The flat or lamellar form of micro-
scopic grains of clay, oxide and slip,
with feldspar helping adhesion of
the slip, those colored slips, oxides, cobalt,
chromium, iron, the peach from copper
   and manganese,
and then you slipped away, great fluxing agent
   causing flow.

That round seat at the round wheel,
seat still and stable, wheel turning, hands
lifting clay upward from beginning
to the end, lifting up, above all, life.

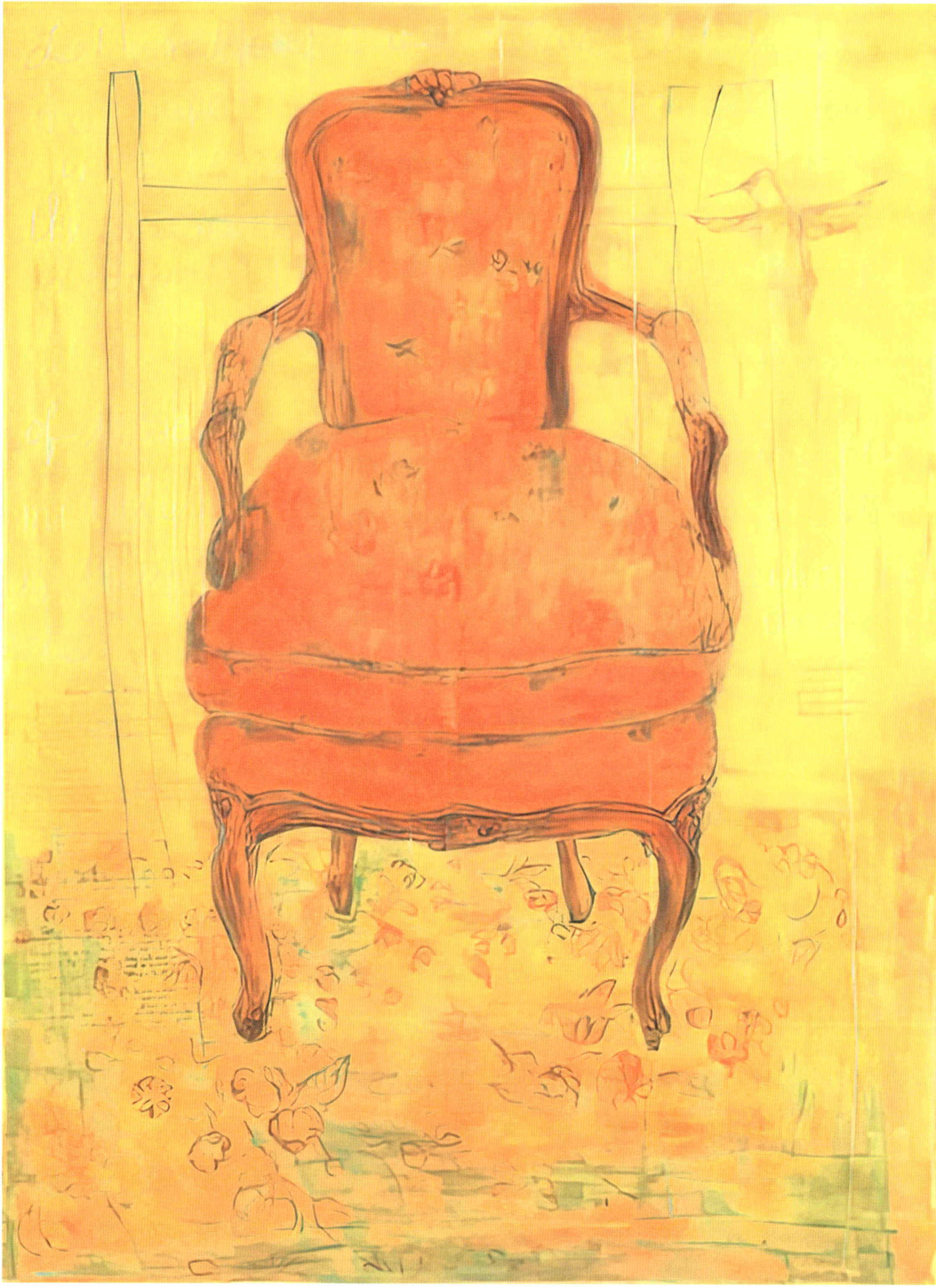

XXV

The long way to go came
and went. That moment's fissure
into the chef's heart, how annealed
the chair that caught him at
day's end, annealed to steady meals
and breaks from all of that.

How reluctant did you, chair,
leave him go, as we did too, in shock,
and would have caught him
could we, cushion him, as in the hardest
times of love and work did you.

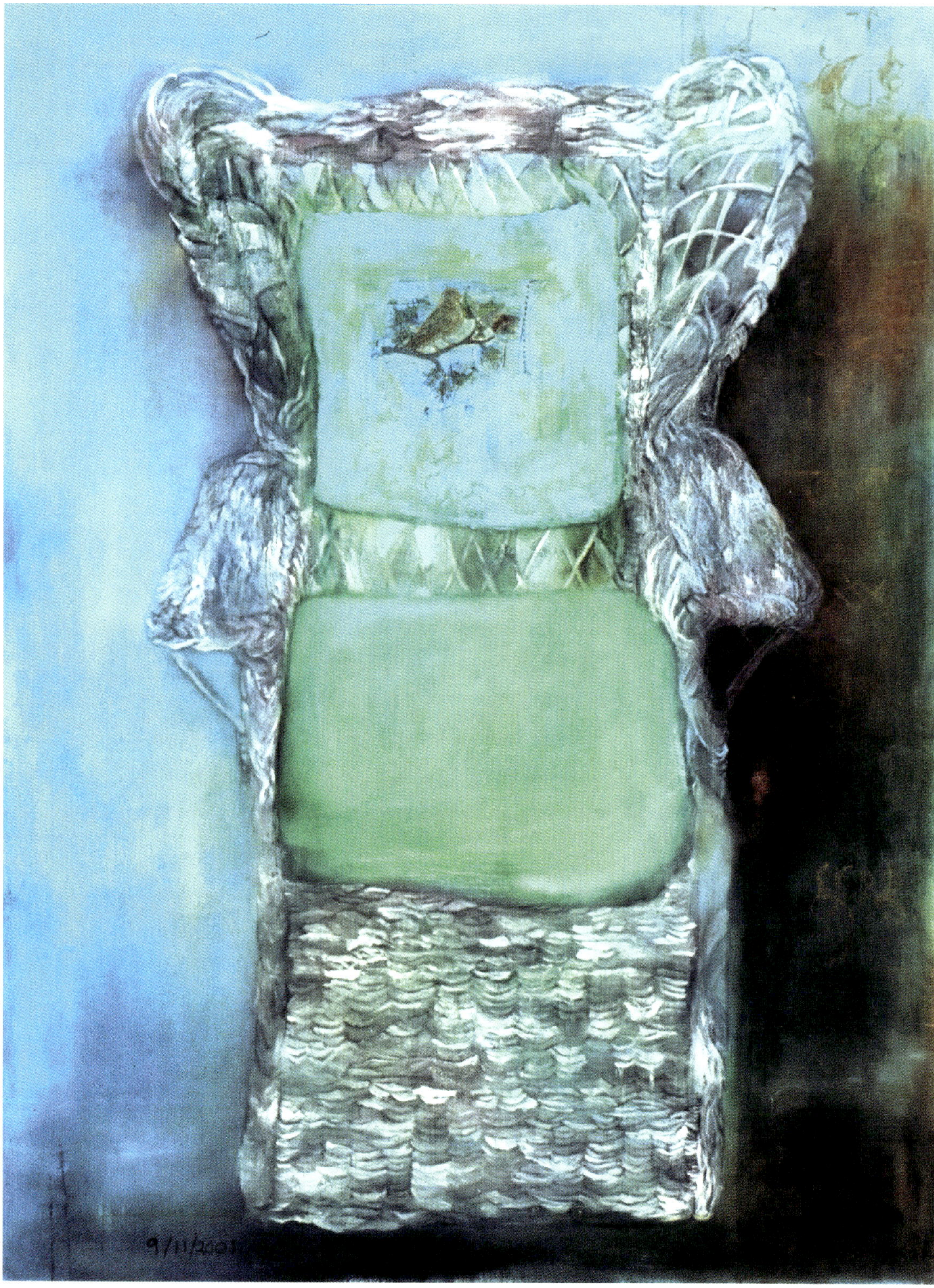
9/11/2003

XXVI

Child's rocker with woven seat,
a rewoven seat, inference of legacy,
of transgenerational heritage
and peace. Rocker bringing

a certain joy where child belongs,
child-sized, too small for griefs or
for primordial miscalculations.
This gift of place so pure and sweet.

Then, outgrown, you rock gently
in the attic breeze, neither dismissive
of the mice and squirrels, nor doubtful
that the child now missed has lost
the drive or purpose learned in you.

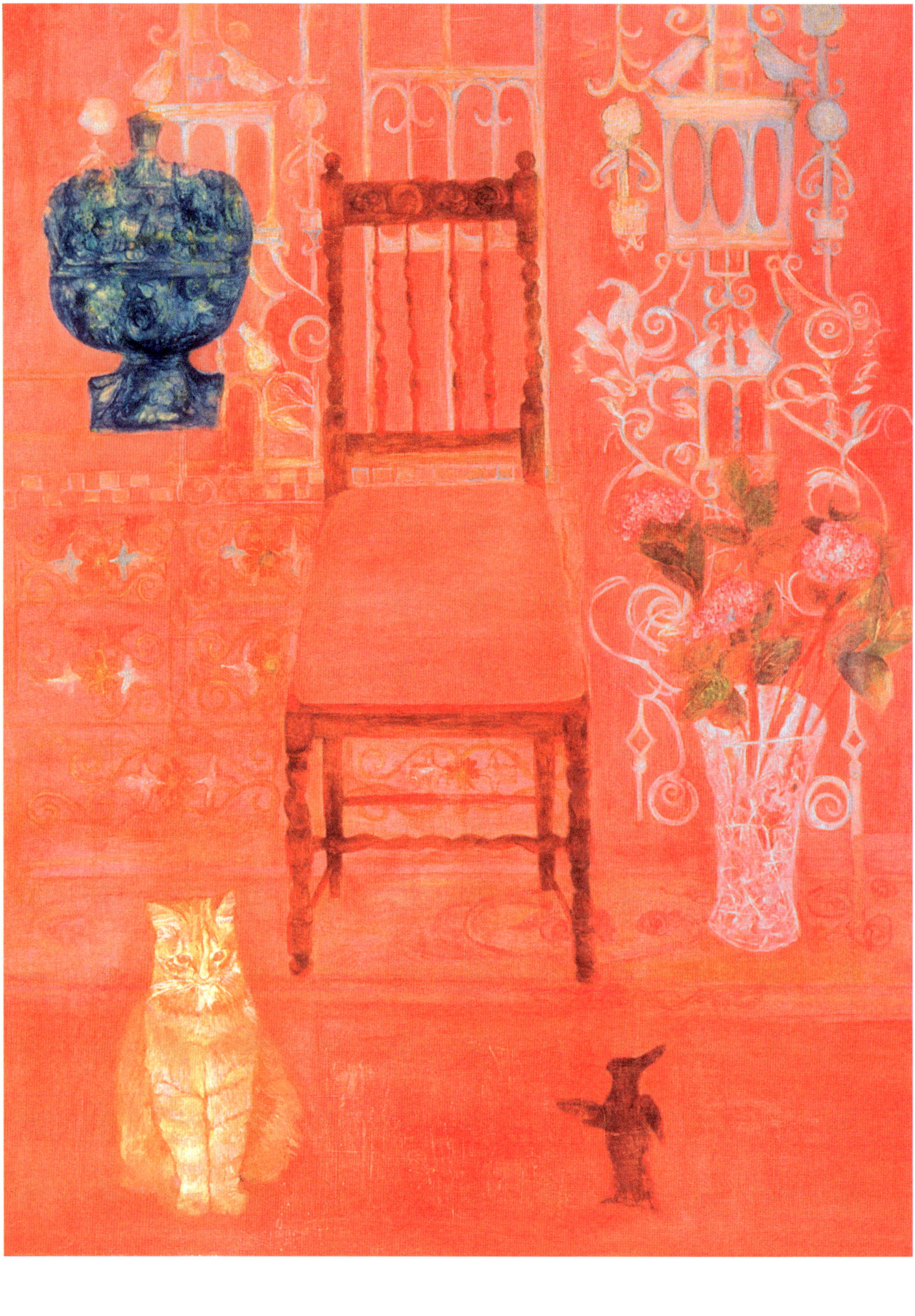

XXVII

Antique chair, guarded like treasure!
Your effort raucous, humble yet essential.
Erratic attention – coffee, tea, gin –
calls for your absolute waiting through
political storms and odd spatial interventions
floating over you, just outside the poor creative reach.

And accolades or acceptances are immaterial
to the translucence irradiating from
you and by association, through the mind,
purposeful in space above you,
and bodied forth out of the fray.

In place, to place, to initiate
in grace, the countless countenances
and the empty space into light
and, without haste, to be the seat of all.

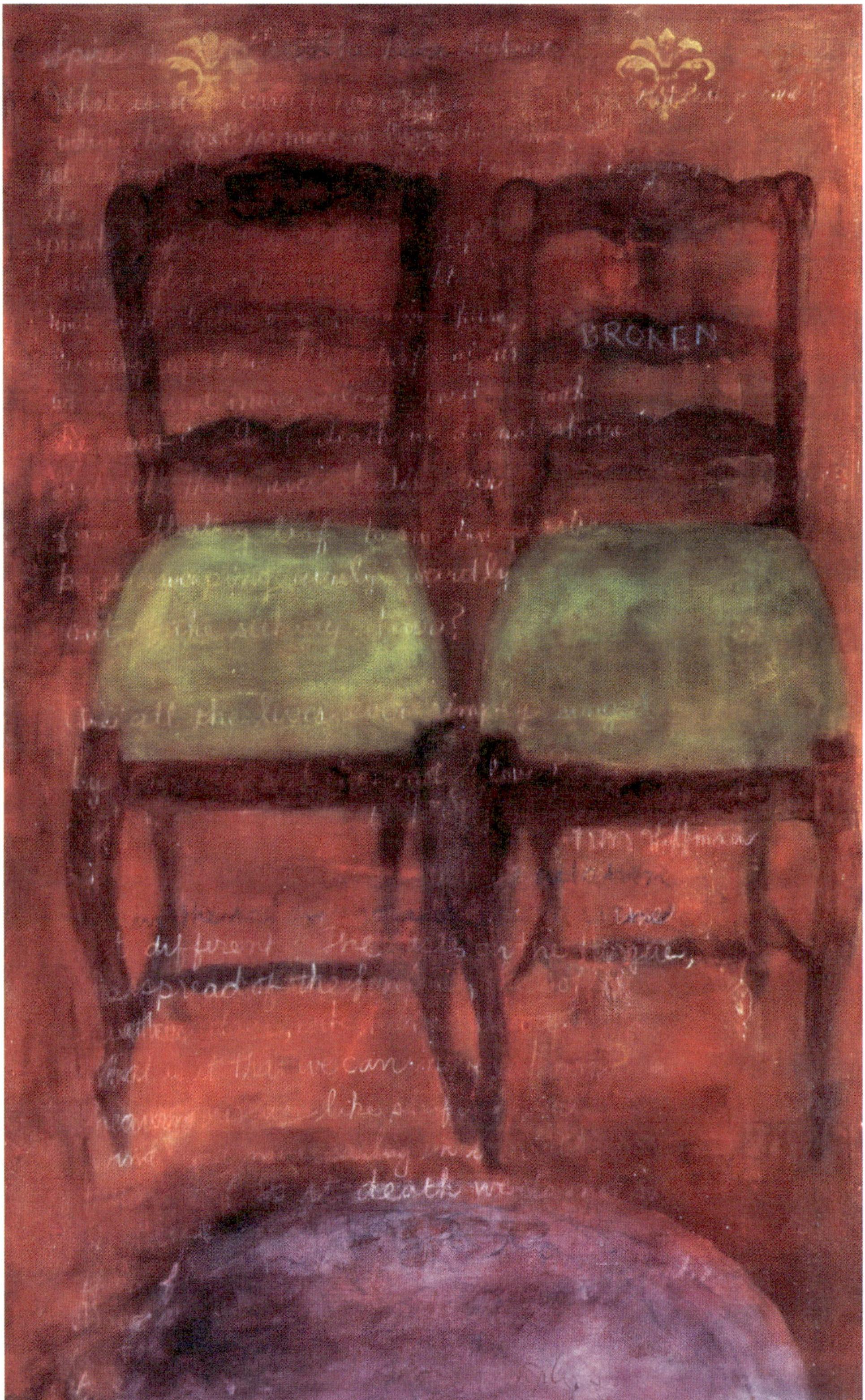
BROKEN

XXVIII

What is it to care, to be in relation
when the root is more or less the same,
yet different? The taste on the tongue,
the spread of the fingers, the soft
leather glove, ink, wine, blood.
What is it that we can never share,
heaving up at us like shafts of air,
wind and mire sailing in it with
the news? Is it death we do not share?
Is it life that never shades over
from floating leaf to swollen plastic
bags sweeping airily, weirdly
out of the subway stair?
Are all the lives ever simply *singed*
by proximity and it is not love?

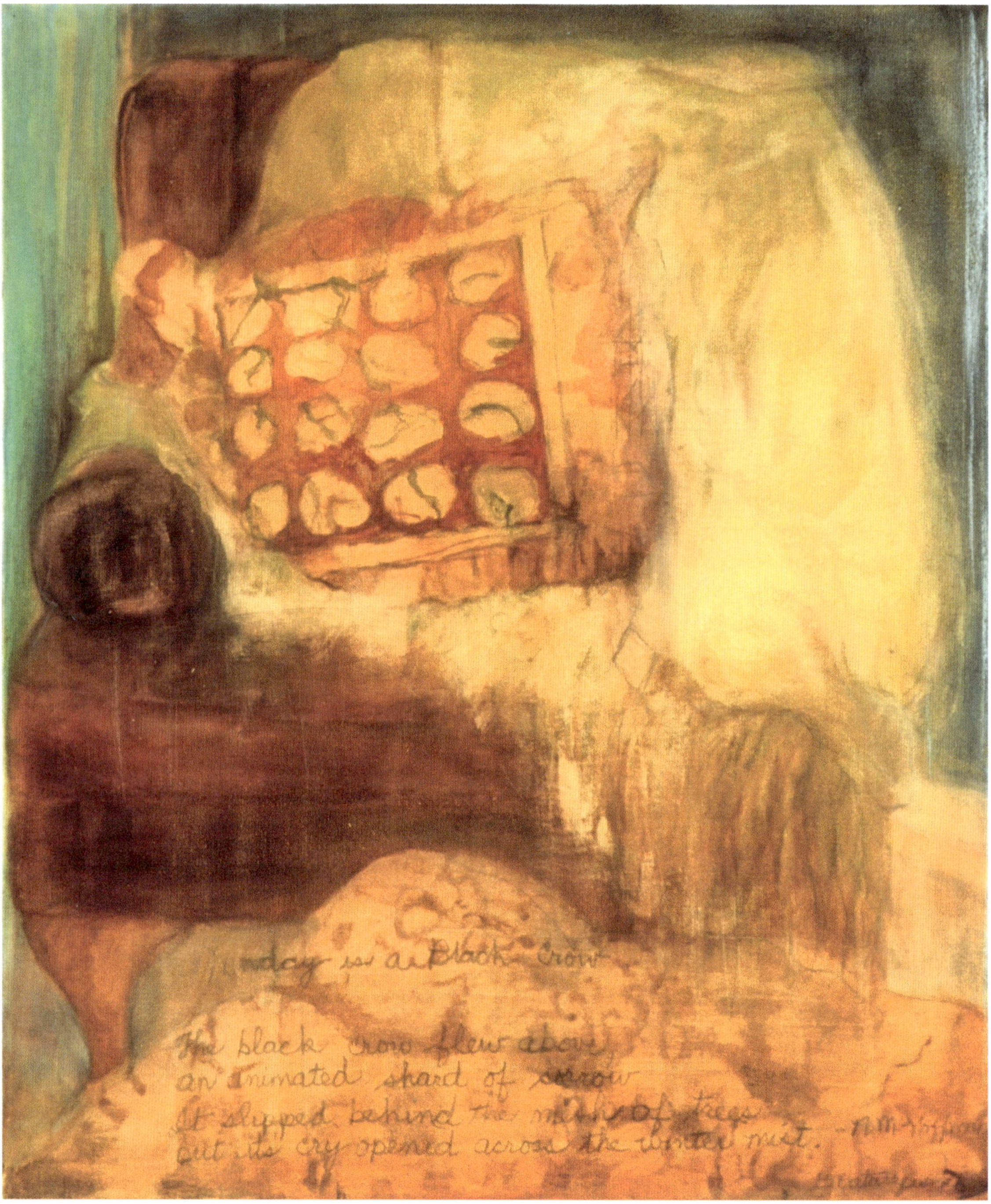
day is a Black Crow
The black crow flew above
an animated shard of sorrow
but its cry opened across the winter mist.

XXIX

The black crow flew above,
an animated shard of sorrow.
It slipped behind the mesh of trees
but its cry opened across the winter mist.

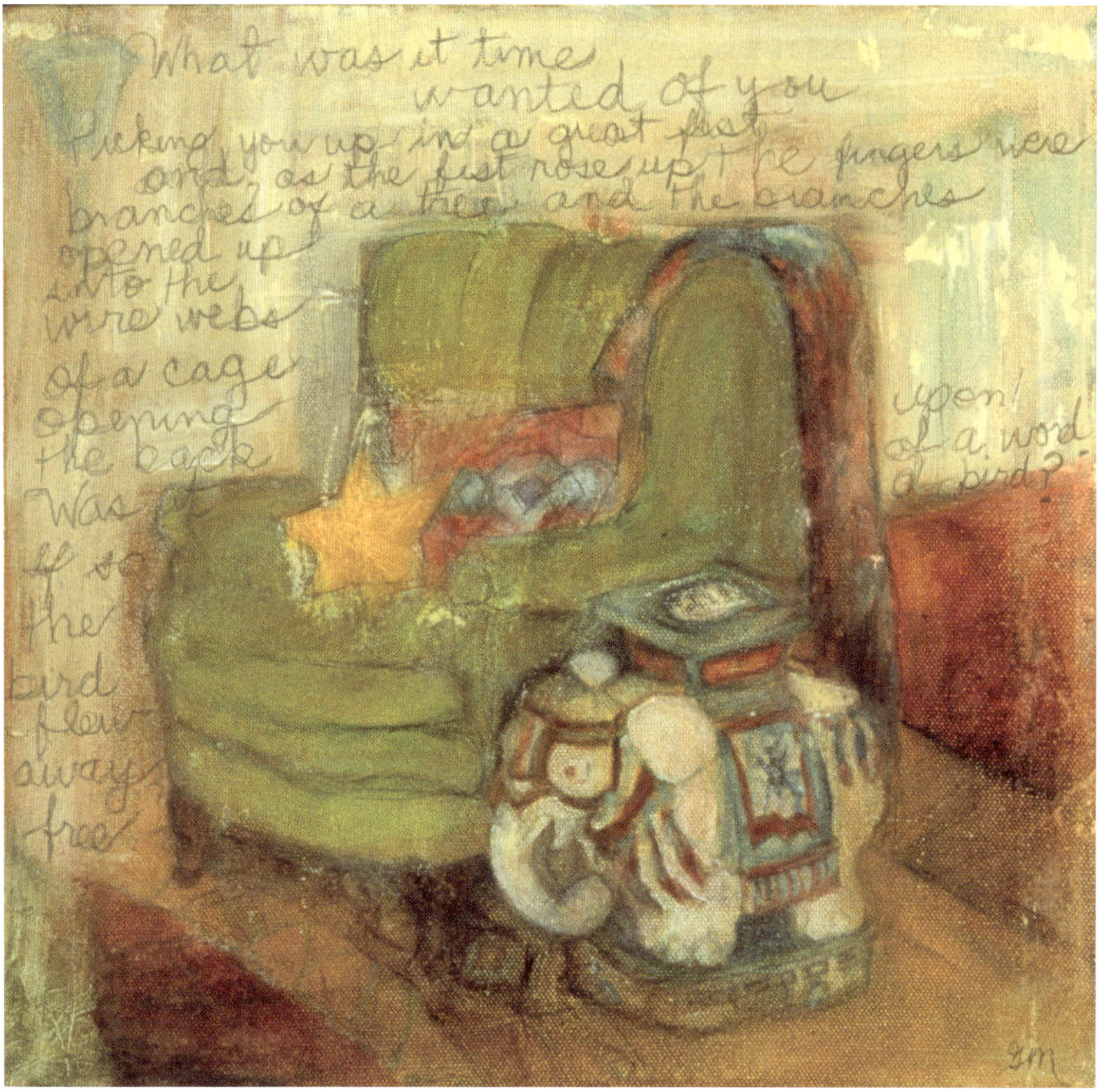
What was it time
wanted of you
Picking you up in a great fist
and as the fist rose up the fingers were
branches of a tree and the branches
opened up
into the
wire webs
of a cage
opening
the back
Was it
If so
the
bird
flew
away
free
upon
of a word
a bird?
GM

XXX

What was it time wanted of you
Picking you up in a great fist
and, as the fist rose up, the fingers were
branches of a tree and the branches opened up
into the wire webs of a cage opening
up on the back of a word. Was it a bird?
If so, the bird flew away, free.

NOTES ON THE POEMS

XI In Memory of Agnes Reiker Hoffmann,
my Austrian grandmother

XIII After Osip Mandelstam and Hannah Arendt

XIV After W. B. Yeats
For Anne Gerety

XV For my mother, Theresa Flannery Hoffman,
in Memory of two of her brothers:
SGM John A. Flannery, who served for three years in Europe with the 104th Infantry "Timberwolf" Division which liberated Nordhausen and the Dora-Mittelbau concentration camps in early April 1945. John witnessed to these events later in life with a Jewish survivor of the Holocaust to students in schools in upstate New York. The 104th Infantry Division was honored as a liberating unit by the U.S. Army's Center of Military History and the United States Holocaust Memorial Museum in 1988.

Cpl. Robert M. Flannery, 17th Airborne Division, 139th Engineering Battalion, Company A, was killed in action on February 6, 1945 after the Battle of the Bulge. Robert was an engineer clearing mines with others in his unit near Hosingen and the River Our.

XVI This poem (*Inviting the Great "Yes" to Sit Down*) is from the gaudiana,* *One Hundred Petal Rose*
For Judith Ann Chambliss

XVII In Memory of Benazir Bhutto
Benazir Bhutto (21 June 1953 – 27 December 2007) was the 11th Prime Minister and 13th Prime Minister of Pakistan from 1988 to 1990 and from 1993 to 1996. She was the first woman to head a democratic government in a Muslim majority country. She was assassinated in 2007, two weeks before the 2008 general election in which she was a leading opposition candidate. Benazir Bhutto was awarded the United Nations Prize in the Field of Human Rights in 2009.

XVIII In Memory of Shoji Hamada
Shoji Hamada (1894-1978), the internationally acclaimed Japanese potter who lived and worked in Mashiko, north of Tokyo, is known to have had a collection of wooden chairs.

XIX Dedicated to New York City hospital workers, particularly Paul Pavese

XX After W. H. Auden and Miguel de Cervantes Saavedra

XXIII In Honor of Eliud Kipchoge
Eliud Kipchoge (born in 1984) is one of the fastest distance runners of all time. He was born in the Nandi District of Kenya and is a Kalenjin of the Talai clan which is a tribe of the Nandi people. The Nandi trace their roots to a particular "orkoiyot" or ritual expert

and community sage from the mid-19th century. All Talai are believed to have been born with special spiritual abilities. The words "Orkoiyot" and "Eliud" figure acrostically in the poem.

XXIV In Memory of Patricia C. Kearns
Thanks to Terry Gess for guidance on ceramics issues.

XXV In Memory of Stephen R. Adamo

XXVI For Miles & Jack and Branson & Caelus

XXVII For Peter Graasbol Schmidt

XXVIII This poem (*Love in the Near Distance*) is from the gaudiana,* *Spire*
For Karen Kurti & Glenn Abrett

XXIX After the painting, *Winter Without a Spring,* by Gloria Matuszewski
For Gloria Matuszewski

XXX For Gloria Matuszewski

* The *gaudiana* is a five-poem form inspired by Antoni Gaudí's architecture. It is blank verse and, like a building of Gaudí's, provides a practical and commodious frame for embellishments.

INDEX OF PAINTINGS

Cover — *Sonoma* (2012) (36″×36″) oil on canvas.
Private Collection.

I — *Chair With Pillow* (1995) (21″×21″) pencil on paper.
Private Collection.
This is the first drawing in the Chair series.

II — *Studio Chair #5* (2002) (30″×22″) oil, pencil on paper. *Private Collection.*

III — *Exit Strategy* (2008) (24″×24″) oil on canvas.
Private Collection.

IV — *Barbara's Chair* (2005) (24″×24″) oil on canvas.
Private Collection.

V — *Chair On Lake Street* (1997) (24″×22″) pencil, oil on gessoed paper. *Private Collection.*

VI — *The Recovered Chair* (1996) (40″×30″) oil, pencil on paper. *Private Collection.*

VII — *Forgiving Chair #1* (2002) (13″×10″) mixed media on paper. *Private Collection.*

VIII — *Studio Chair #4* (1996) (42″×30″) oil, pencil on paper. *Private Collection.*

IX *Chartreuse Chair* (2003) (24″×20″) oil on canvas. *Private Collection.*

X *New York City Chair* (2002) (60″×44″) oil on canvas. *Private Collection.*

XI *Studio Chair #2* (1994) (12″×9″) encaustic, oil on canvas. *Private Collection.*

XII *Study For A Chair* (2008) (25″×19″) pencil, oil on gessoed paper. *Private Collection.*

XIII *Studio Chair #7* (2007) (12″×12″) encaustic, oil on canvas. *Private Collection.*

XIV *Where Are You Judy True?* (2004) (44″×60″) encaustic, oil on canvas. *Private Collection.*

XV *Magenta Chair* (2002) (60″×40″) oil on canvas. *Private Collection.*

In Memory of my father, Louis S. Mattis, who received the Silver Star, the Bronze Star and the Purple Heart for his service in World War II.

Magenta, *an early aniline dye, was so named as a color on account of its discovery soon after the June 4, 1859 battle between Austrian and Franco-Sardinian troops near Magenta, Italy. The choice of the word Magenta for the new color (formerly* fuchsine or roseine*) highlighted the association between the dye's blood-red color and that bloody battle.*

XVI *Forgiving Chair #2* (2002) (13″×10″) mixed media on paper. *Private Collection.*

XVII *Prayer #11* (1999) (51″×50″) oil, mixed media on canvas. *Private Collection.*

XVIII *November Chair* (2005) (24″×24″) oil on canvas. *Private Collection.*

XIX *In The Name Of* (2004) (72″×60″) oil, encaustic, mixed media on canvas. *Private Collection. Written into the painting are names of Iraqi civilians and American soldiers who died in Operation Desert Storm.*

XX *Studio Chair #3* (1995) (21″×21″) oil, pencil on paper. *Private Collection.*

XXI *The Three Chairs* (1996) (28″×50″) oil, pencil on paper. *Private Collection.*

XXII *Where Are You Judy True?* (2004) (44″×60″) encaustic, oil on canvas. *Private Collection (detail).*

XXIII *Forgiving Chair #3* (2002) (13″×10″) mixed media on paper. *Private Collection.*

XXIV *Chair For A Lady* (2003) (24″×18″) oil on canvas. *Private Collection.*

XXV *Susan's Recipe* (2001) (60″×44″) oil, mixed media on canvas. *Private Collection. In Memory of my mother, Susan Pereksta Mattis.*

XXVI *And the Singing Bird Will Come* (2001) (60″×44″) oil, mixed media on canvas. *Private Collection. This painting was finished on September 11, 2001.*

XXVII *The Pink Painting* (2006) (60″×44″) oil on canvas. *Private Collection.*

XXVIII *Two Chairs* (2003) (60″×36″) oil, encaustic on canvas. *Private Collection.*

XXIX *Chair With Ottoman* (2001) (24″×20″) oil, mixed media on canvas. *Private Collection.*

XXX *The Murray Chair* (2001) (12″×12″) oil, mixed media on canvas. *Private Collection.*

Published in 2024 by Kearns, Howard & Walker

www.nmhoffman.com

www.gloriamatuszewski.com
ISBN: 978-1-7354615-1-9

The Chairs was printed on Munken Polar paper 150 g/m²
produced by Arctic Paper Munkedals, Sweden.
Printing was done in February 2024 by Média Graphic
in Rennes, France, using Led-UV offset printing technologies.
The slipcase was produced by Média Graphic with Materica
paper produced by Fedrigoni, Italy

Art photographed for reproduction by
Jay Daniel / Black Cat Studio / Novato, California

Photoengraving by
La Photogravure du Sphinx / Montreuil, France

The Chairs is typeset in Sainte Colombe,
designed by Yoann Minet

The first printing is
four hundred books, all slipcased

Book design by Élie Colistro
www.eliecolistro.com

KEARNS, HOWARD & WALKER is the publishing arm of the Hubert H. & Elsie Lui Family of Students, originally established in Chicago in 1968 and subsequently based in San Francisco and the Bay Area from 1979 to the present. Based in the states of California, New York, Oregon, Virginia, and Washington ∾ United States of America

www.khwpublisher.com